Children's Health and Illness Recovery Program (CHIRP)

PROGRAMS THAT WORK

✓PROGRAMS THAT WORK

Children's Health and Illness Recovery Program (CHIRP)

CLINICIAN GUIDE

BRYAN D. CARTER

WILLIAM G. KRONENBERGER

ERIC L. SCOTT

CHRISTINE E. BRADY

OXFORD
UNIVERSITY PRESS

OXFORD
UNIVERSITY PRESS

Oxford University Press is a department of the University of Oxford. It furthers the University's objective of excellence in research, scholarship, and education by publishing worldwide. Oxford is a registered trade mark of Oxford University Press in the UK and certain other countries.

Published in the United States of America by Oxford University Press
198 Madison Avenue, New York, NY 10016, United States of America.

Library of Congress Cataloging-in-Publication Data
Names: Carter, Bryan D., author. | Kronenberger, William G., author. |
Scott, Eric L. (Eric Lee), author. | Brady, Christine E., author.
Title: Children's health and illness recovery program (CHIRP) :
clinician guide / Bryan D. Carter, William G. Kronenberger,
Eric L. Scott, Christine E. Brady.
Description: New York, NY : Oxford University Press, [2020] |
Series: Programs that work | Includes bibliographical references and index.
Identifiers: LCCN 2019048681 (print) | LCCN 2019048682 (ebook) |
ISBN 9780190070267 (paperback) | ISBN 9780190070281 (epub) |
ISBN 9780190070298
Subjects: LCSH: Chronically ill children–Life skills guides. |
Chronic diseases in adolescence—Psychological aspects. |
Chronically ill children—Mental health. | Chronically ill children—Family relationships.
Classification: LCC RJ380 .C377 2020 (print) | LCC RJ380 (ebook) | DDC 618.92/044—dc23
LC record available at https://lccn.loc.gov/2019048681
LC ebook record available at https://lccn.loc.gov/2019048682

9 8 7 6 5 4 3 2 1

Printed by Marquis, Canada

To my wife Amy, children, and grandchildren

—BDC

To David and Cassie

—WGK

To the memory of Henry

—ELS

To my partner in everything, Justin

—CEB

About PROGRAMS THAT WORK

Stunning developments in healthcare have taken place over the past several years, but many of our widely accepted interventions and strategies in mental health and behavioral medicine have been brought into question by research evidence as not only lacking benefit, but perhaps inducing harm (Barlow, 2010). Other strategies have been proved effective using the best current standards of evidence, resulting in broad-based recommendations to make these practices more available to the public (McHugh & Barlow, 2012). Several recent developments are behind this revolution. First, we have arrived at a much deeper understanding of pathology, both psychological and physical, which has led to the development of new, more precisely targeted interventions. Second, our research methodologies have improved substantially, such that we have reduced threats to internal and external validity, making the outcomes more directly applicable to clinical situations. Third, governments around the world and healthcare systems and policymakers have decided that the quality of care should improve, that it should be evidence-based, and that it is in the public's interest to ensure that this happens (Barlow, 2004; Institute of Medicine, 2001, 2015; Weisz & Kazdin, 2017).

Of course, the major stumbling block for clinicians everywhere is the accessibility of newly developed evidence-based psychological interventions. Workshops and books can go only so far in acquainting responsible and conscientious practitioners with the latest behavioral healthcare practices and their applicability to individual patients. This series, Programs *ThatWork*™, is devoted to communicating these exciting new interventions for children and adolescents to clinicians on the frontlines of practice.

The manuals and workbooks in this series contain step-by-step detailed procedures for assessing and treating specific problems and diagnoses. But this series also goes beyond the books and manuals by providing ancillary materials that will approximate the supervisory process in assisting practitioners in the implementation of these procedures in their practice.

In our emerging healthcare system, the growing consensus is that evidence-based practice offers the most responsible course of action for the mental health professional. All behavioral healthcare clinicians deeply desire to provide the best possible care for their patients. In this series, our aim is to close the dissemination and information gap and make that possible.

This clinician guide is the go-to resource for implementing the Children's Health and Illness Recovery Program (CHIRP). This initiative synthesizes treatments from a variety of disciplines and is founded on family-based treatment principles, leading to successful interventions for adolescents coping with chronic illness. Strongly rooted in evidence-based practice, research has shown that the CHIRP treatment program has resulted in higher measures of feelings of independence and an overall decrease in symptoms of fatigue and chronic pain experienced by youth who have participated in the program. With this manual, clinicians will be equipped with the necessary tools to work within the interconnected team of physicians, specialists, and other healthcare professionals who are crucial components of long-term treatment of this population.

—Anne Marie Albano, Editor-in-Chief
—David H. Barlow, Editor-in-Chief
Programs *ThatWork*

References

Barlow, D. H. (2004). Psychological treatments. *American Psychologist, 59*, 869–878.

Barlow, D. H. (2010). Negative effects from psychological treatments: A perspective. *American Psychologist, 65*(2), 13–20.

Institute of Medicine. (2001). *Crossing the quality chasm: A new health system for the 21st century.* Washington, DC: National Academy Press.

Institute of Medicine. (2015). *Psychosocial interventions for mental and substance use disorders: A framework for establishing evidence-based standards.* Washington, DC: National Academy Press.

McHugh, R. K., & Barlow, D. H. (2012). *Dissemination and implementation of evidence-based psychological interventions.* Oxford: Oxford University Press.

Weisz, J. R., & Kazdin, A. E. (2017). *Evidence-based psychotherapies for children and adolescents* (3rd ed.). New York: Guilford.

Accessing Treatments *ThatWork* Forms and Worksheets Online

All forms and worksheets from books in the PTW series are made available digitally shortly following print publication. You may download, print, save, and digitally complete them as PDFs. To access the forms and worksheets, please visit http://www.oup.com/us/ttw

Contents

Acknowledgments

We would like to express our appreciation for the contributions of numerous colleagues who have reviewed various versions of the Handbook and Workbook (Gerard Banez, Dennis Drotar, Michelle Ernst, Anne Lynch-Jordan, Carl von Bayer, and others), postdoctoral fellows (Heather Bass, Sandy Bowersox, Elaine Gilbert, Shannon Hartley, Kristen Milazzo, Isabelle Oh, Jenny Petrie, Kristin Rabineau, Kristie Vail Schultz, Katherine Kiker Sherman, Sarah Cruce Spurling, and Aimee Townsend Thompson), research assistants (Jessica King Bailey, Melanie Bierenbaum, Lara Jones, Danielle Mizzell, Kate Price, Alex Pruitt, Katherine Daniels Schwartzkopf, Morgan Springer, and Brooke Threlkeld), and the innovative clinicians and researchers who have graciously permitted us to adapt aspects of their work in tailoring the CHIRP interventions to address the needs of youth and their families coping with the challenges of chronic illness. Most importantly, our thanks go to our many teens and their families who have helped us develop and refine this program. In particular, we would like to thank the Barbara Blair Foundation, the Barr Foundation and the Petersdorf Norton Healthcare Community Trust Foundation, Norton Children's Hospital, and Norton Healthcare for their generous support and funding of various stages of research and project development.

—BDC, WGK, ES, and CB

Introduction and Prep Session

Adolescents with chronic illness, particularly when accompanied by debilitating, painful, and/or fatiguing symptoms, face challenges that may prove disruptive to their normal physical, psychological, and social developmental trajectories (Pinquart & Teubert, 2012; Wysocki et al., 2006). The Children's Health and Illness Recovery Program (CHIRP) is an interdisciplinary family-based treatment program designed to maximize the functioning of teens with chronic illness. It was developed from both a careful review of the evidence-based literature on treatment programs for adolescents with chronic physical illness and the authors' more than six decades of combined experience in helping children and families improve their quality of life and independence while coping with pediatric illness. Early versions of many CHIRP components, including handouts that have been updated for the CHIRP program, have been used clinically by the authors and others for many years and have been described in other publications (e.g., Kronenberger & Dunn, 2009).

This CHIRP Clinician Guide provides detailed instructions for implementing the manualized treatment protocol in the CHIRP Teen and Family Workbook. The Clinician Guide attempts to go beyond the Workbook by informing the clinician as to the philosophy, pragmatics, and art of working with these challenging pediatric populations. Additionally, the Clinician Guide provides the tools needed to establish a collaborative treatment team approach that incorporates the skills of the CHIRP clinician, primary care and specialty physicians, and the various other health care (e.g., physical therapists, occupational therapists) and educational professionals critical to the successful management and treatment of these youth.

In CHIRP, since most of the adolescents seen for treatment are also medical patients with chronic health conditions, we sometimes use the term "patients" in referring to them, *particularly when communicating with their physicians and health care providers*. For the purposes of this Clinician Guide, when we use the terms "youth," "teen," "adolescent," or "patient," we are referring to an "adolescent with a chronic medical condition."

The Impact and Challenges of Pediatric Chronic Illness

About This Program

The reading level and content of the Workbook have been intentionally geared toward addressing the challenges faced by adolescents (typically ages 12–18) with a chronic health condition and their parents/families. Additionally, the evidence supporting the CHIRP intervention as an effective treatment for the functional deficits that many of these teens present is based on our research with an adolescent patient population, as is much of the research behind the treatment approaches we have adapted to the Workbook (e.g., behavioral family systems therapy [BFST] research with adolescent diabetic patients). Clinically, we have found it useful to employ elements of CHIRP with bright younger patients, and our goal is to eventually create parallel developmentally sensitive resources for preadolescents.

It is also important to note that while CHIRP has been developed to address the broad array of issues confronting teens with chronic health conditions, many of the intervention strategies are designed to impact the frequently encountered problems these youth have with persistent pain, fatigue, and somatic symptoms that may become associated with their illness state. It is our experience in treating these patients that these issues often contribute the most to their functional disability and thus need to be specifically targeted to create maximum therapeutic improvement. Therefore, this Clinician Guide will frequently reference research and clinical literature pertinent to addressing these clinical conditions as key components to improving adolescent chronic illness coping and adjustment.

For consistency, we refer to the primary caregiver of the teen as the parent/parents. This acknowledges the functional role that these adults play in the life of the adolescent while recognizing that these primary caregivers can be custodial relatives such as grandparents, as well as nonrelated adoptive parents and foster parents.

Illness-Specific and Non–Illness-Specific Factors

Chronic health conditions can impact child and adolescent functioning in multiple domains including physical, cognitive, psychological, social, emotional, and educational (Suris, Michaud, & Viner, 2004). However, the type of illness may differentially impact on and involve the body in various ways. For instance, spina bifida primarily involves the central nervous system (CNS), a condition like cystic fibrosis (CF) will primarily impact pulmonary/respiratory and digestive functioning, while diabetes involves the endocrine system and affects multiple domains such as growth and cognitive skills. Thus, it is naïve to assume that all chronic illnesses impact children and teens in the same way. A recent meta-analysis (Pinquart & Teubert, 2012) elucidated the differential impact that different illnesses can have. For example, some illnesses, such as diseases of the CNS, are more likely to impact physical mobility and/or cognitive functioning. Other illnesses, such as chronic fatigue syndrome, greatly impact energy level and time spent in accomplishing daily tasks. A number of chronic illnesses such as cancers and congenital heart conditions may involve intense treatments for an extended period of time, which severely limits the child's ability to socially interact with peers in normal academic and recreational settings. However, regardless of the degree of challenge experienced in any one of these areas, the goal of treatment remains the same: to increase recovery of function in order to maximize the attainment of important developmental milestones.

Interaction of Teen Illness with Patient and Family Functioning

Having an adolescent with a chronic illness can have a major impact on parent–teen and family dynamics. The *transactional stress and coping model* (Thompson, Gil, Burbach, Keith, & Kinney, 1993) conceptualizes chronic disease as a stressor to which teens and families must adapt. While the model includes medical indices, strong emphasis is placed on teen and parent psychosocial variables, including parent variables such as overall adjustment, social support, stress, and cognitions regarding adolescent development and health. Within this domain, parental beliefs may play a major role in mediating the impact of the teen's illness on parental behaviors. It has been found that increased parental perception of child vulnerability is related to increased social anxiety in the child, even when controlling for child age and disease severity (Schanberg, Anthony, Gil, & Maurin, 2003). Parental education and psychological sophistication are related to both increased perceptions of child vulnerability and increased school absences (i.e., parental decision to keep the child home from school). Parental anxiety and concerns about their teen's health may lead parents to restrict involvement in school and social activities and often leads to a maladaptive pattern of parent–teen interactions and decision-making, including extent of health care utilization (Bush & Iannotti, 1990). In their study of adolescents with inflammatory bowel disease (IBD), Reed-Knight et al. (2017) found greater family stress to be positively related to children's pain-related expressions of distress and passive coping, suggesting that family stress can place children at risk for greater expressed pain-related distress through effects on coping and depressive symptoms. Therefore, developing interventions aimed at addressing family-based psychosocial difficulties is important for enhancing teen adjustment to chronic illness: interventions must target the family system—the parents as well as their adolescent (and siblings). In this regard, health providers need to assess and address parental beliefs and parenting practices in granting age-appropriate independence to the teen in managing both their illness-related and non–illness-related life skills.

Psychological Adjustment Issues in Pediatric Chronic Illness

While many youth with chronic illness are well adjusted psychosocially, a sizable number may be at increased risk for developing adjustment difficulties including depression, anxiety, and problems in peer relationships (e.g., Noll, LeRoy, Bukowski, Rogosch, & Kulkarni, 1991). Youth with chronic illnesses often miss school due to illness-related complications, medication side effects, and hospitalizations, which likely leads to anxiety about getting behind in school work and social anxiety due to their long absences from age-appropriate social activities due to illness-related restrictions (Wallander & Varni, 1998). Understandably, these missed developmental experiences can contribute to the development of a negative self-concept and lack of self-confidence in both academic and social arenas critical to acquiring autonomy as adolescents approach adult life, along with their accompanying mood difficulties. Indeed, addressing the unique concerns, stresses, goals, and dynamics of adolescents with chronic health conditions and their families is critical to maximizing their successful transition to adult life.

Academics and Vocational Success

Adolescents with chronic illnesses often must confront a number of school stressors not experienced by their healthy peers. Such adolescents are likely to have decreased school attendance due to hospitalization, have to administer necessary medical treatments during the school day, attend medical/therapy appointments that interrupt their school day, and tolerate physical symptoms and limitations that may detract from their focus and performance (Eiser, 1997; Suris et al., 2004). Some medical conditions and/or associated medications and treatments may result in extreme fatigue, pain, impaired concentration, short-term memory, executive function deficits, and visual/auditory perception problems (Shapiro & Manz, 2004). Such presenting problems can often be addressed through open communication with the school regarding the teen's presenting diagnosis and course of treatment (Suris et al., 2004), as well as advocating for necessary and appropriate accommodations to ensure that the teen is able to attend and function to the best of their ability at school (Shapiro & Manz, 2004; Smith & Carter, 2004). Beyond academic attendance and performance, chronic illnesses can also have an impact on the adolescent's future vocational success and their ability to function independently (Suris et al., 2004). CHIRP addresses these issues as a component to intervention by working with patients and their families in providing written 504 Plan (Rehabilitation Act of

1973) recommendations for accommodations specific to the child and their illness/disability.

Social Impact

Chronic illness can greatly impact social interactions in adolescents. Some teens with a chronic illness may differ in appearance from their peers (e.g., using the aid of a wheelchair) or have to administer treatments that may seem unfamiliar to peers (e.g., checking blood glucose, using an inhaler, injections), which can lead to negative self-concept, low self-confidence, alienation, or even bullying. In addition, youth with chronic illness also have increased time away from their peers due in part to hospitalizations, medical appointments and treatments, decreased school attendance, and illness-associated fatigue, which results in decreased interactions with same-aged peers (Eiser, 1997; Suris et al., 2004). Teens with chronic illness are also more reliant on their parents for assistance with managing their chronic conditions, which may further restrict time with other teens and interfere with attaining developmentally critical mastery of independence and self-confidence. However, despite these challenges, it is imperative to create awareness of issues affecting peer interactions and encourage teens to initiate and maintain peer relationships to increase their independence and foster growth (Suris et al., 2004).

Functional Disability Model for Pediatric Chronic Illness

Williams and Zahka (2017) emphasize the need for addressing the confluence of the biomedical with the biopsychosocial model of pediatric illness, particularly in those clinical scenarios where the primary focus of patient and family is on somatic symptoms to the detriment of maximizing patient functioning in meeting critical developmental milestones. Figure I.1 illustrates a proposed dynamic-interactive explanatory model underlying the development of increasing functional disability in teens with a chronic illness (Carter, Edwards, Kronenberger, Michalczyk, & Marshall, 1995). From the perspective of this model, teens with a chronic health condition may have predisposing factors or

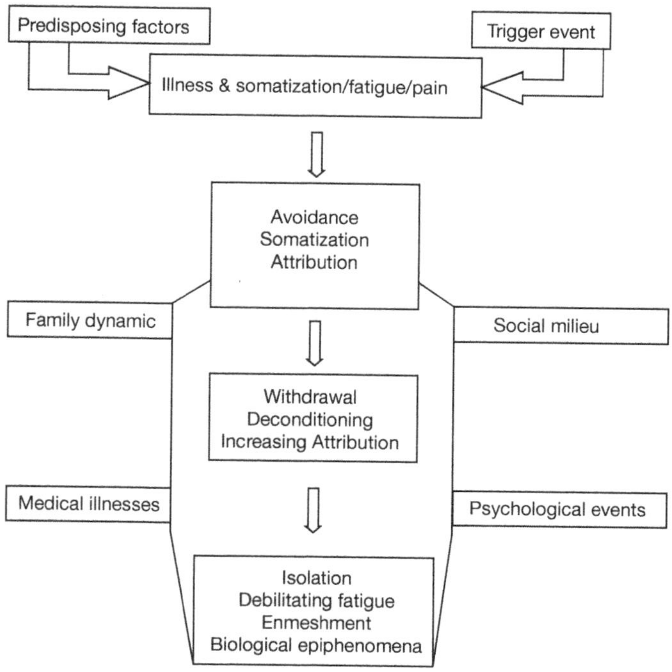

Figure I.1

Dynamic-interactive model for increasing functional disability in adolescent chronic illness.

vulnerabilities which, when combined with overt or covert trigger events (e.g., viral illness, psychological stress), result in an initial illness with associated somatic symptoms, often including pain and/or fatigue. This may lead to the patient engaging in avoidance of activity, somatization (increased vigilance to physical symptoms), and attribution of the illness primarily toward events outside their control. Influenced by additional events such as family dynamics (e.g., overprotection, triangulation), social milieu factors (e.g., peer relationship conflicts), other medical illness (e.g., low-grade infections, pain/fatigue, illness exacerbations), and psychological events (e.g., catastrophizing cognitions), the patient may engage in further withdrawal, deconditioning, and increasing attribution that their illness/debilitation is due solely to a unitary disease process for which there is a unitary passive treatment (e.g., medication or surgery). The final pathological outcome is a teen who experiences increasing social isolation, debilitating pain and fatigue, enmeshment with their family/primary caregivers, and additional biological epiphenomena that further reinforce a primary somatic symptom-relief focus.

CHIRP Treatment Approach

The CHIRP treatment approach is based on the following *key foundations*:

- *Developing a chronic-treatable (vs. acute-curable) illness perspective.* A primary emphasis is placed on helping adolescents and parents understand that their illness is a chronic condition that can be treated and managed, as opposed to an acute illness that can be quickly cured. This decreases the sense of desperation and reduces the hopelessness that often comes from dashed expectations that the next specialist will have a "magic bullet" remedy. It also deemphasizes rapid symptom reduction and focuses on gradual improved functioning, which is a much more realistic and achievable goal in most chronic pediatric conditions.
- *Embracing a "coping" approach.* Depending on the patient's medical condition, improved functioning will often take time and sustained effort. It is important to emphasize that the acquisition of coping and stress management skills is essential for improved functioning and quality of life. Increasingly, the research supports a treatment approach emphasizing acceptance and learning to live and function in the presence of symptoms rather than efforts aimed primarily at eliminating symptoms (Dahl, Wilson, & Nilson, 2004; Lipani & Walker, 2005; McCracken, 1998).
- *Moving from a state of functional disability to functioning.* It is helpful for the patient and family to recognize that the illness has resulted in a dysfunction in the regulation of the body's ability to manage or control a number of functions, including energy level, pain sensitivity/tolerance, sleep, memory, concentration, etc. This involves an explanation of how the condition likely evolved and is exacerbated by a host of physical, environmental, emotional, and behavioral factors. Recovery is focused on comprehensive activities designed to gradually facilitate the adolescent in returning to more normal functioning.

- *Resuming increased approximations to "normalcy."* Recovery of functioning is facilitated by the teen gradually resuming and maintaining approximations to more "normal" involvement in academic, social, and physical/recreational activities as soon as possible. This includes the eventual goal of returning to school, which is critical to the teen's increased feelings of "normalcy." Prolonged school absenteeism isolates the adolescent from normal social contacts, often resulting in increased social anxiety and avoidance. Furthermore, it may promote identification primarily with the sick role and add to the teen's stressors when faced with excessive academic make-up work or even having to acquire specialized educational services (e.g., under a 504 Plan).
- *Importance of adopting an organized program of graduated exercise and activity.* It is paramount that teens be involved in some form of medically guided, appropriately increased physical activity therapy (for some, this may include formal physical and occupational therapy) and an exercise regimen that emphasizes increasing strength and flexibility while promoting graduated aerobic conditioning. Unnecessary prolonged bed rest and physical inactivity is strongly discouraged since these promote further deconditioning, which is likely to perpetuate somatic symptoms. A graduated exercise program should be implemented as soon as possible in the patient's treatment program, and this is often done in coordination with a physical therapist or rehabilitation program (Williams & Zahka, 2017). A useful analogy is the fact that athletes generally do not simply wait for an injury to totally heal before returning to their sport. Instead, they engage in a process of returning to full participation by gradually increasing their exercise and practice.
- *Family-based cognitive behavioral intervention.* There is a growing body of evidence supporting specialized family-based cognitive behavioral therapies (cognitive behavioral therapy [CBT], BFST) and derivations from CBT such as motivational interviewing (MI) and acceptance and commitment therapy (ACT). These are interventions to facilitate the adolescent's coping with both illness-related and non–illness-related stressors and managing of family dynamics so as to deemphasize inadvertent identification with and reinforcement of illness behaviors.

- *Coordinated medical management of the patient's illness and symptoms.* Medically, specific therapies such as nonsteroidal anti-inflammatory agents for headache and musculoskeletal pain, selective serotonin reuptake inhibitors for anxiety or depressive symptoms, sleep agents for more severe sleep disturbances, and the like may be needed adjunctively to improve individual target symptoms.
- *Improved sleep behavior.* Sleep difficulties should be given careful attention as many teens with chronic illness have severe problems with sleep latency, unrefreshing sleep, late awakening, and prolonged daytime naps and are at risk of developing sleep-phase abnormalities. This may be exacerbated when patients have been placed on home-hospital/home-bound or home schooling and normal daytime schedules and routines are disrupted. In fact, in families with a child with chronic illness, often the entire family has altered their sleep schedules and even sleeping arrangements based on the child's illness issues, thus necessitating and reconfiguring sleep hygiene for the whole family (Williams & Zahka, 2017).
- *Interdisciplinary collaboration, coordination, and communication.* Perhaps most importantly, all of these treatment elements need to be integrated and coordinated to minimize therapeutic misadventures and maximize the confidence of the patient and family in the treatment process. An open and communicative therapeutic relationship is often the foundation of a successful treatment program.
- *Employing a developmental perspective.* The CHIRP intervention emphasizes the critical importance, even in the context of chronic illness, of setting developmentally appropriate goals for the teen and facilitating the attainment of critical experiences in their physical, academic, psychological, and social development.

The components forming the foundation of CHIRP are represented in Figure I.2. It is important to emphasize that to maximize the adolescent's improvement in functioning, it is necessary to focus efforts on improving physical activity, academic attendance and performance, social involvement and competence, and an overall approach to lifestyle management and coping that appropriately interfaces with the teen's health condition. Like a four-legged table, there must be equal emphasis if there is to be balance in the teen's functioning.

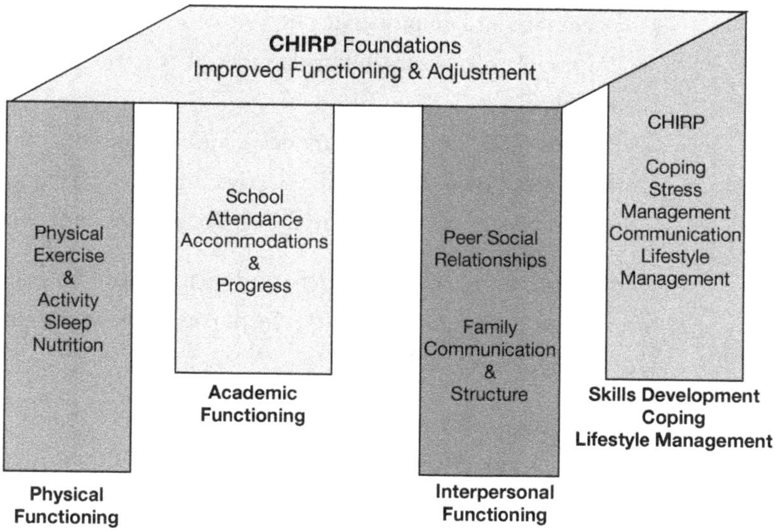

Figure I.2

Four foundations of the Children's Health and Illness Recovery Program (CHIRP).

Fostering Critical Developmental Experiences

It is crucial to emphasize to the parents/guardians of adolescents with a chronic illness the importance of their teen having as normal developmental experiences as allowable in the context of their chronic health condition. The following guidelines should be frequently presented to families to encourage them to adopt and promote increasing independence in the teen's daily life:

- Provide increasing opportunities for growth and development (social, educational, industry/productivity).
- Provide a safety net by meeting basic needs (security).
- Provide the teen with structure by making and enforcing clearly defined rules and expectations while also involving teens in developing and revising their schedule.
- Set and maintain expectations and boundaries in order to emphasize the importance of balance ("want to" vs. "have to").
- Set up a division of responsibilities within the household and enforce it.
- Hold the teen accountable for setting and meeting goals in order to build confidence and competence.
- Encourage and reinforce teen independent behaviors.

- Encourage and demonstrate effective communication skills.
- Promote family values in how family activities and commitments are organized.
- Perhaps most importantly, model adaptive behaviors for the teen in the parent's own life, including active problem solving and self-care (vs. a model of self-sacrifice in the service of meeting the teen's needs).

At the same time, both the parent and teen need to be made aware of the teen's role and responsibilities in pursuing increasing independent functioning. These include:

- Following family rules and responsibilities.
- Learning to effectively and assertively communicate needs and feelings while also becoming an effective listener.
- Gaining increasing independence in effectively managing health needs, including exercise, treatments, medications, diet, balanced sleep, making and keeping appointments, and so on.
- Maintaining reasonable and balanced involvement in activities outside the home, including friends, school, recreation, church/temple/mosque, etc., and with family.
- Discussing and appropriately addressing mood and motivation issues in the management of the teen's lifestyle.
- Developing a reasonable yet flexible schedule while avoiding over- and/or underactivity with consideration for changing medical condition factors.
- Supporting and encouraging other family members.

Throughout the course of treatment in CHIRP, it is helpful to revisit these two lists with the patient and family in order to continually emphasize that these are *critical* developmental tasks that must be accomplished if the adolescent is to successfully transition to adulthood and responsibly manage their health condition while pursuing meaningful life experiences and goals.

Intervention Approaches Incorporated in CHIRP

Cognitive Behavioral Therapy and Related Approaches

CBT is perhaps the most well-validated nonpharmacological treatment for facilitating coping and adjustment in youth with chronic illness, pain, and fatigue (Christie & Wilson, 2005; Eccleston et al., 2014). Cognitive behavioral treatment approaches have been shown to alter patient symptom-related beliefs (attributions) and, subsequently, level of functional disability (Jensen, Turner, & Romano, 2001). Demonstrated benefits of CBT include reductions in anxiety, depressive, and somatic symptoms, which frequently co-occur in patients with chronic illnesses involving persistent pain and fatigue (Kashikar-Zuck, Goldschneider, Powers, Vaught, & Hersey, 2001; Palermo, 2012; Williams & Zahka, 2017). In particular, *catastrophic thinking* (a form of "strong belief" in CHIRP terminology), a prime target of CBT interventions, has been associated with poorer outcome and greater functional disability in patients with chronic pain (Lynch, Kashikar-Zuck, Goldschneider, & Jones, 2006). When applied in the context of CHIRP, teen and parent belief systems in the following arenas are the most frequently addressed:

TEEN:

- Adhering to the belief that one must restrict activity and involvement until all symptoms resolve.
- Struggling with self-image and confidence in interpersonal relationships.
- Accepting and employing assertive communication and behavior in their relationships with peers, adults, and family.
- Placing overemphasis on peer acceptance and "pleasing others."
- Addressing the setting of appropriate and realistic standards for achievement and success.
- Becoming overly dependent on others in order to manage and/or recover from illness exacerbations.
- Difficulty in overcoming feelings of invalidation when others do not seem to understand or accept their illness.
- Pessimism regarding future health outcome and personal success.

PARENT/GUARDIAN:

- Being hesitant to promote increased activity and independence for fear of worsening patient symptoms.
- Fearful of teen relapse, leading to overprotection and overreaction to even minor symptoms or exacerbations.

- Being preoccupied by future projection of teen failure and incapacitation due to illness.
- Believing that the adolescent is "faking" or exaggerating symptoms.

Szigethy and colleagues (2007) employed a cognitive behavioral intervention to reduce anxiety and depressive symptoms in youth with IBD, as well as to improve their perception of increased control over their disease management. CBT has been shown to improve physical functioning, reduce fatigue severity, and increase school attendance compared to a wait-list control group in adolescents with chronic fatigue syndrome (CFS; Stulemeijer, de Jong, Fiselier, Hoogveld, & Bleijenberg, 2005). CBT approaches that focus on addressing cognitive and lifestyle barriers via increased patient exposure to social, school, and leisure related activities and scheduled short walks and tasks carried out at intervals throughout the day have also improved function in adolescents with CFS (Chalder, Godfrey, Ridsdale, King, & Wessely, 2003). Breaking the association between experiencing symptoms and stopping activity (i.e., avoidance), self-monitoring of functional improvements, establishing a consistent sleep routine, and using anticipatory relapse prevention are other components of these CBT interventions. Kashikar-Zuck and colleagues (2005) treated 30 patients with juvenile fibromyalgia syndrome (JFMS) in a randomized controlled trial (RCT) study comparing an eight-session CBT intervention to self-monitoring. At posttreatment subjects were crossed over into the opposite treatment arm for 8 weeks, ensuring that all adolescents eventually received both CBT and self-monitoring. While both treatment conditions showed a significant decrease in depressive symptoms and functional disability, those receiving CBT demonstrated significantly greater ability to cope with pain than those in the self-monitoring only condition. All adolescents had significantly lower levels of functional disability and depressive symptoms compared to baseline, but those who received self-monitoring followed by CBT seemed to receive the most benefit.

Family Systems Intervention

A number of therapeutic activities incorporated into the CHIRP intervention are derived from BFST (Wysocki, Harris, Greco, Mertlich, & Buckloh, 2001). BFST is an evidence-based, structured approach designed to enhance parent–adolescent communication and problem-solving skills targeting parent–adolescent conflict around chronic illness and treatment-related issues. Therapeutic interventions involve helping family members to more objectively identify communication difficulties and teaching them both general and disease-specific problem-solving and conflict resolution skills in order to generate more helpful alternatives.

BFST addresses how to effectively handle conflicts between adolescents and their parents through a comprehensive, time-limited approach, typically lasting 10 sessions. While this therapy approach can be applied to any adolescent and their relationship with their parent, Wysocki, Harris, Greco, Mertlich, and Buckloh (2001) have compiled a treatment manual to apply BFST specifically for adolescents with chronic illnesses. Their family treatment approach consists of the BFST cornerstones of problem solving (e.g., behavior contracts), communication skills training (e.g., recognizing communication patterns), and cognitive restructuring (e.g., identifying strong beliefs), which they employ in a 12-session structure. BFST with adolescents with poorly controlled type 1 diabetes and their families has been shown to increase positive adolescent–parent interactions as measured both by self-report and observed behavior (Wysocki et al., 1999, 2000). Wysocki and colleagues have now extended BFST to specifically address the care of adolescents with type 1 diabetes in BFST for Diabetes (BFST-D), which includes targeting diabetes-specific behaviors in an extended treatment period (6 months), training in behavioral contracting, and a parental simulation of having diabetes for 1 week. BFST-D has been shown to not only decrease family conflict, but also improve treatment adherence in adolescents with type 1 diabetes (Wysocki et al., 2006, 2007).

CHIRP has adapted components of the BFST approach within treatment to decrease adolescent–parent conflict and increase positive communication, improve problem solving, and implement cognitive restructuring, all of which serve the goal of increasing teen independence in disease and lifestyle management. Psychoeducation, feedback, modeling, rehearsal, and behavioral homework assignments are all employed in treatment sessions. Cognitive restructuring is used to modify extreme or counterproductive attitudes and "strong beliefs" that parents and adolescents may hold about each other and that lead to conflict, alienation, and decreased adolescent self-confidence in independence strivings. Multiple systems are incorporated into the therapeutic approach including, as needed, the family, the school, and the medical team. From a family systems perspective, problems are conceptualized as arising from problematic family structure and role functions that can impede effective communication and problem solving. Within the CHIRP model, these dynamics are often conceptualized as arising from the "slippery slope" of parents failing to adapt from an acute illness perspective (primarily comforting and protecting) in responding to their child's illness to a chronic illness perspective (facilitating coping and independence in the context of the child's health status). The elegance of the BFST model in addressing developmentally relevant issues in chronic illness coping is in the integration of cognitive behavioral and family systems perspectives into a cohesive and ecological therapeutic approach.

Sleep Intervention

Sleep disturbance is prominent in pediatric patients with chronic conditions, particularly when fatigue and pain are involved, and it has been associated with more difficulties with mood and behavior (Aaltonen, Hamalainen, & Hoppu, 2000; Degotardi et al., 2006; Huntley, Campo, Dahl, & Lewin, 2007; Hysing, Sivertsen, Stormark, Elgen, & Lundervold, 2009; Mitchell, Kopel, Williams, Cespedes, & Bruzzese, 2015; Long, Krishnamurphy, & Palermo, 2008; MacAllister et al., 2009; McCarthy, Bastiani, & Williams, 2016; Meltzer, Logan, & Mindell, 2005; Miller, Palermo, Powers, Scher, & Hershey, 2003; Sivertsen, Hysing, Elgen, Stormark, & Lundervold, 2009; Snodgrass, Harvey, Scheinberg, & Knight, 2015; Stinson et al., 2014; Sumpter, Dorris, Kelly, & McMillan, 2013; Tsai et al., 2008; Walter, Nixon, Davey, Downie, & Home, 2015; Williams & Zahka, 2017). Disrupted sleep may be related to a variety of factors including health condition symptoms such as pain and fatigue; schedule changes associated with decreased school attendance, home-hospital/home-bound, or home schooling; diminished social and activity involvement; stress; a perception of loss of control over health; more permissive parenting in the face of a serious illness; and family struggles (in the present digital age) around the use of electronics and social media. Furthermore, disrupted sleep in a child with a chronic illness can clearly negatively impact parent sleep as well (Meltzer & Montgomery-Downs, 2011).

Resolution of sleep disturbances can play an important role in the recovery process (Degotardi et al., 2006; Williams & Zahka, 2017). When chronic pain is involved, the relationship between pain and sleep is bidirectional: insufficient or disrupted sleep may increase the level of pain experienced, and chronic pain increases the likelihood of sleep disruption (Lewin & Dahl, 1999). Disturbances in sleep in children have been shown to be a major contributor to fatigue symptoms, increased pain intensity, decreased health-related quality of life, and decreased functioning (Huntley et al., 2007; Long et al., 2008; Palermo & Kiska, 2005). A cognitive behavioral program of structured sleep intervention has been demonstrated to improve symptoms and quality of life in adolescents with primary juvenile fibromyalgia and in pediatric cancer survivors (Degotardi et al., 2006; Zhou, Vrooman, Manley, Crabtree, & Recklitis, 2017) and is clearly indicated in children with cancer-related pain and other chronic illnesses (Crabtree, Krishna, & Gozal, 2008; Walter et al., 2015).

The CHIRP intervention targets monitoring sleep behaviors and improving sleep hygiene over the course of treatment because this area of functioning is often disrupted in adolescents with chronic illness who are often at home and possibly bedridden due to illness and avoidance of activity.

Graduated Exercise and Activity

Research has demonstrated that increased physical activity and exercise is a critical component to recovery from pediatric conditions involving functional disability, pain, or fatigue (Anthony & Schanberg, 2005). Graduated exercise and activity have been included in a number of integrative treatment programs, and many investigations have underscored its importance. Black and colleagues (2017) have developed the Fibromyalgia Integrative Training for Teens (FIT Teens) intervention, which combines CBT with specialized neuromuscular exercise training modified from evidence-based injury prevention protocols and employed it in a small-group intervention (16 sessions over 8 weeks). FIT Teens was determined to be feasible, well-tolerated, and safe for adolescents with chronic pain and functional disability associated with JFM. Those completing the treatment reported enjoying the group format, increased self-efficacy, increased strength, and improvement in their motivation to exercise. Participants also reported decreased pain and increased energy levels, which of course can contribute to improved sleep. A treatment manual is being developed from this work. FIT Teens targets improvement in confidence in movement and activity participation.

Viner and colleagues (2004) employed a program for adolescents with CFS involving graduated levels of physical activity and exercise along with parental and medical support. Treatment was shown to reduce overall severity of fatigue symptoms, with 43% of patients reporting complete resolution of CFS symptoms compared to only 4.5% of those having supportive care alone. Wellness scores and school attendance were improved over those of supportive care cohorts at a 2-year follow-up. Many chronic illness conditions involve disabling symptoms of fatigue that often lead to patient inactivity and deconditioning, suggesting that graduated increases in activity and exercise should be an integral component of any intervention targeting improved functional ability. It is important to note that when working with pediatric patients with pain and fatigue associated with certain well-delineated medical conditions (e.g., leukemias, chronic renal disease, and sickle cell disease), more aggressive physical therapy approaches may be contraindicated. However, a structured physical activity program individually tailored to the teen's limitations can facilitate increases in physical, psychological, social, and academic functioning.

Finally, it is important to remember the clinical implications of research showing that intervention effects diminish over time, making it unrealistic to expect adherence-promoting interventions to have long and lasting effects (Kahana, Drotar, & Frazier, 2008). Interventions promoting adherence to such lifestyle changes as increased exercise, activity, and sleep need to be an ongoing part of the clinical management of pediatric chronic illness.

Educational and Academic Accommodations and Advocacy

Adolescents with chronic illnesses often face a number of stressors related to academics. For example, youth with chronic illnesses are likely to have decreased school attendance, which may be due to hospitalization, necessary medical treatments, attending medical/therapy appointments, or not feeling well enough to attend school (Eiser, 1997; Suris et al., 2004). They may also have trouble concentrating or experience fatigue or pain (Shapiro & Manz, 2004). Such presenting problems can be addressed with open communication with the school regarding the teen's presenting diagnosis and course of treatment (Suris et al., 2004), as well as advocating for necessary and appropriate accommodations to ensure that the teen is able to attend and function to their best ability at school (as per the Individuals with Disabilities Education Act [IDEA]; see Shapiro & Manz, 2004; Smith & Carter, 2004; Williams & Zahka, 2017). Such accommodations may be available through a 504 Plan or an Individualized Education Plan (IEP). These accommodations are provided to youth with a physical or mental condition to ensure that they are not penalized for their conditions but are instead given the opportunity to achieve in an educational setting. In addition to academics, chronic illnesses can also have an impact on adolescents' future vocational success and their ability to function independently (Suris et al., 2004), which makes early intervention (by using 504 Plans, for example) even more important for the success of the teen not only now, but in the future as well.

Ideally, school reintegration is accepted as an important component central to the functional recovery process and serves as a therapeutic experience for both adolescent and family. Patients may vary in the level of social and academic impairment they exhibit. Some continue to attend school only to experience extreme exhaustion at the end of the day that precludes them from engaging in family and peer socialization or recreational activities and may interfere in keeping up with homework and out-of-class assignments. Others have not attended school for weeks, months, or even years by the time they present for treatment, with many being home-schooled or receiving home-hospital/homebound instruction. In light of these variations, school reintegration is a highly individualized process based on teen, family, and school structure as well as needs/resources. Some teens strongly resist the return to school. In such cases, school avoidance may stem from overt stressors such as peer harassment, ostracism, or falling behind in academic work. For others, there are long-standing and impairing social anxieties that predate the onset of current symptoms and have remained hidden or masked by more pressing symptoms; these may reveal themselves later in treatment, when return to school is a distinct possibility. Parents may harbor their own anxiety about teens returning to school and may support the teen in delaying reentry.

The level of clinician involvement in advocating for the teen's educational needs varies considerably based on a number of factors. School reentry is multifactorial in that it serves as a measure of treatment success, as a treatment goal, and as an intervention in and of itself. From a treatment perspective, even a return to partial day attendance provides the teen with opportunities for practicing key skills involved in CHIRP (e.g., improving and expanding peer relationships, improving communication, applying problem-focused coping skills, engaging in assertive behaviors and self-advocacy, and communicating with others about their illness and need for accommodations). These are all valuable and important to the teen's coping and recovery over the course of an extended illness.

Many patients and parents indicate that the clinician's advocacy and active involvement in working with the school to educate school personnel about the teen's specific condition and orchestrating accommodations appropriate to their illness served as a pivotal point in the "joining" process of treatment (Kazak, Simms, & Rourke, 2002). As such, the clinician serves as a representative of the multidisciplinary treatment team in interpreting the teen's illness to school personnel, providing examples of patient- and illness-specific accommodations, attending IEP/504 Plan meetings, providing needed documentation to support academic interventions, and so on.

School systems vary widely in their receptiveness to recommended accommodations and interventions. Therefore, it is important that you become familiar with the appropriate federal and state regulations and statutes that apply to these pediatric health conditions, such as the IDEA (Smith & Carter, 2004). If a child fails to qualify for an IEP and still requires some accommodations and modifications to fully participate in the classroom, they may need accommodations under Section 504 of the Rehabilitation Act and the Americans with Disabilities Act, which require some accommodations and modifications be made so that the student can fully participate in the classroom and maximally benefit from educational instruction. Appendix A: Model 504 Letter, in this Clinician Guide provides an example of a letter to a patient's school to initiate the process of establishing a working advocacy relationship.

Interdisciplinary Collaboration and Communication

It is the goal of CHIRP to form a collaborative network of knowledgeable and understanding health care and educational professionals who will treat the adolescent and family with respect as collaborators in the process of improving patient health, independent functioning, and quality of life. In this process it is important to emphasize the following principles and practices:

1. Emphasis is on patient *functional improvement* rather than a "cure."
2. *Open communication* between all professionals, teachers/school staff, etc.
3. *Consolidation of medical care* under a single physician when possible.
4. *Close working relationship* with primary care physician and/or referring specialist is essential; written communication should include a comprehensive management plan (refer to Appendix E: CHIRP Interdisciplinary Communication Form and Appendix F: CHIRP Feedback Forms).
5. *Regularly scheduled medical visits* should *not* be contingent on symptom/illness exacerbation in order to reassure the patient and family that concerns have not been dismissed and that ongoing medical events will be addressed.
6. It is important to *clearly define criteria for medically excused school absences* and to designate which physician or health care provider is responsible for verifying excused school absences, including the assignment of patients to home-hospital/home-bound instruction for clearly delineated periods of time.
7. The *CHIRP clinician may serve as the bridge* between the school and patient/family, managing absences and accommodations (504 Plan; IEP).

The CHIRP approach utilizes a variety of methods to accomplish the goal of truly interdisciplinary communication and collaboration. One specific strategy involves the use of faxable and/or emailed program forms (see Appendix D: CHIRP Physician Referral Form; Appendix

E: CHIRP Interdisciplinary Communication Form; and Appendix F: CHIRP Feedback Form) that include the fax numbers and email addresses of all involved health care professionals. This is designed to ease the process of faxing these forms back and forth among treating professionals and maximize interdisciplinary communication, rather than relying on patient/family report of what each professional said. In many instances the electronic medical record may be the main device through which to share information among health care providers. Of course, all privacy and confidentiality principles must be adhered to in the process of conducting interdisciplinary communication.

It is often beneficial to have an interdisciplinary care conference, in person or via conferencing, with the patient and family early in the course of treatment with CHIRP. This may be difficult for some professionals to coordinate if they do not practice in the same facility or setting. However, the benefits can be extremely valuable to prevent splintering of services and possible miscommunication among professionals and with the patient/family.

The interprofessional approach of CHIRP is intended to encourage and maintain ongoing communication among all of the patient's health care providers and educators that will aid in supporting symptom reduction and a return to normal daily functioning. It cannot be overemphasized that careful coordination and regular communication are often crucial to obtaining a lasting successful outcome. While the interprofessional communication forms and provider fax information provided by the Clinician Guide may be beneficial, more integrated care (or at minimum face-to-face collaborative discussions on a regular basis) are likely to be more effective. Evaluation and treatment of adolescents and their families meeting the challenges of chronic illnesses necessitate a comprehensive interprofessional approach. Highly effective communication and collaboration among treatment team members is associated with increased patient satisfaction and engagement as well as patient disease-specific outcomes.

Empirical Support for CHIRP

Many of the components of CHIRP have been validated in the treatment of pediatric patients with chronic illness, pain, fatigue, and functional disability as presented elsewhere in this Guide. CHIRP represents our efforts to operationalize and integrate these validated treatments with additional interventions designed to maximize patients' return to more normal functioning in the multiple areas critical to adolescent development.

Carter, Kronenberger, Threlkeld, Townsend, and Pruitt (2013) conducted a study of a series of clinical referrals for CHIRP intervention (*N* = 26; 25 female, 1 male; age 11–19 years; mean [M] = 15.6, standard deviation [SD] = 1.8) with chronic medical conditions involving painful and fatiguing symptoms (primary diagnoses included postural orthostatic tachycardia syndrome, dysautonomia, fibromyalgia, CFS, chronic headaches, complex regional pain syndrome, and functional pain with nonepileptic psychogenic seizures; many subjects met criteria for more than one condition, with chronic fatigue being the most frequent secondary comorbid condition). Patients and parents completed measures before and after the 12-session manualized CHIRP intervention for symptoms of pain (Pain Severity Scale [PSS], Parent- and Self-Report Forms, 9 items assessing pain; Krupp, LaRocca, Muir-Nash, & Steinberg, 1989), fatigue (Fatigue Severity Scale [FSS], Parent- and Self-Report Forms, 9 items assessing fatigue; Krupp et al., 1989), functional disability (Functional Disability Inventory [FDI], Parent- and Self-Report Forms, 15 items assessing ability to participate in typical daily activities; Claar & Walker, 2006; Walker & Greene, 1991), and treatment helpfulness (rated on a 1–10 scale, with 10 as most helpful). Patients reported significant decreases in pain, fatigue, and functional disability (see Appendix J: CHIRP Outcomes Studies Results), as well as highly favorable ratings of the "helpfulness" of the CHIRP intervention in improving symptoms (M = 7.38) and overall daily functioning (M = 8.71, SD = 1.5). Parent-report ratings of their teen's pain, fatigue, and functional disability decreased significantly. Parent ratings of the "helpfulness" of the CHIRP intervention were highly favorable for improvement of patient symptoms (M = 7.90, SD = 2.4) and overall daily functioning (M = 8.70, SD = 1.9). These results demonstrate that patients completing the CHIRP manualized intervention experienced a significant reduction in pain, fatigue, and functional disability, by both parent and teen report, with effect sizes in the medium to large range. Parents and teens also give the CHIRP intervention high ratings in "helpfulness" both in improving symptoms and overall functioning.

These improvements may lead to decreased health care utilization and improved self-management and coping.

In a longitudinal follow-up of 17 adolescent patients and their parents who completed CHIRP (17 out of 26 CHIRP completers were located and completed measures via phone interview with a researcher; mean duration since completing CHIRP was 2.1 years), both patients and parents/guardians not only reported maintaining the significant improvements made in reported symptoms of pain, fatigue, and functional disability from pretreatment to immediately postintervention, but overall demonstrated continued improvement from immediately postintervention to long-term follow-up (see Appendix K: CHIRP Follow-Up Study Results). This suggests that the skills gained in the CHIRP intervention likely play a role in facilitating the resumption of a more developmentally normal trajectory from young adolescence to older adolescence and young adulthood.

To identify the characteristics of pediatric patients who completed participation in CHIRP versus those who dropped out of treatment prematurely, Carter and colleagues (2015) compared the preintervention profiles of referred adolescents with chronic health conditions. Preintervention demographic characteristics and ratings of pain, fatigue, functional disability, coping style, health beliefs and behaviors, sleep, and parent/teen dynamics were compared between adolescents who either completed (42 total; 39 females, 3 males) or prematurely discontinued (25 total; 19 females, 6 males) the 12-session manualized treatment. Participants who dropped out of treatment were more likely to be male and have a history of repeating a grade in school. Parents of adolescents who dropped out of treatment were more likely to minimize the impact of symptoms on adolescent functioning and report that their teen was less likely to employ active problem-solving coping and have more comorbid medically unexplained conditions, more mood problems, and more sleep difficulties. Adolescents who dropped out of treatment reported being more sensitive/reactive to stress and were more likely to use medications to help them sleep. Certain demographic and individual patient characteristics and family dynamics appear to impact treatment attrition to a manualized cognitive behavioral and family systems intervention for adolescents with chronic pain. These findings suggest the need for developing strategies for strengthening patient and family commitment to a psychosocial approach to chronic pain coping and recovery.

In a case series of three adolescent females with chronic illness seen in a CHIRP intervention conducted in a 12-week separate teen and parent group format (Carter, Schultz, Gilbert, Kronenberger, & Scott, 2018), all three teen participants demonstrated moderate positive changes on weekly self-report items detailing mood, sleep, and overall functioning. Parent participants indicated positive pre- to posttreatment changes for their teens in the areas of mood, sleep, and overall severity of impairment on the Impairment Rating Scale (IRS). The parent participants also completed the PedsQL Family Impact Module, which measured parent and family functioning, where higher scores indicate better functioning. Parents of two of the teens reported positive changes from pre- to postintervention on indices of their own Physical Functioning, Emotional Functioning, and Family Relationship scales over the course of the group. Parent rating of the third teen was not included in analysis due to different raters completing the forms (i.e., father preintervention and mother postintervention).

Additional studies of CHIRP intervention with adolescents with chronic illness are being conducted, including an online telepsychology group intervention with adolescents with CF (Kroll, 2019), chronic motor tic disorders (Vater et al., 2019), and our own ongoing group-based clinical service with adolescents with a wide variety of chronic illnesses at Norton Children's Hospital and the University of Louisville School of Medicine Department of Pediatrics.

Current Limitations of the CHIRP Intervention and Future Research Needs

Research and clinical experience have repeatedly acknowledged that adolescents with medically unexplained symptoms, including chronic pain, are at high risk to drop out of any psychological treatment. In fact, CHIRP retention rates of 65–70% in some of our outcome studies with purely clinical referral populations exceed expectations given the intensity of the CHIRP program and the difficulty of working psychologically with this population. One pilot study at another institution (Kroll, 2019) utilizing CHIRP with a group of adolescents with CF who could see each other via a video connection on a provided iPad (CF patients are discouraged from physical contact due to risk of transmission of highly contagious infections) demonstrated the efficacy of this modality in decreasing attrition from treatment. We are already finding that conducting CHIRP in a teen and parent group format is improving patient ethnic diversity. Hopefully future studies will elucidate other methods for improving inclusiveness and adherence.

As in our study of adolescent patients who dropped out of the CHIRP intervention prematurely (Carter et al., 2015), a recent comprehensive review of evidence-based treatment programs for chronic pain confirmed that there are multiple factors impacting the initiation and completion of treatment, including demographic characteristics, individual patient characteristics, parent characteristics, and family dynamics (Palermo, Wilson, Peters, Lewandowski, & Somhegyi, 2009). There is a great need to develop strategies for strengthening patient and caregiver commitment to manualized treatment programs such as CHIRP, to better identify readiness to change separately in patients and caregivers (Guite et al., 2011), and to identify patients who would benefit from more intensive or less intensive treatment options. Clearly, research designed to identify the most critical variables among the list of factors contributing to treatment attrition (and ways to address them) is needed.

Additional variables to investigate in future studies include program evaluation and cost utility. These include an assessment of the demand for CHIRP, cost (including cost-effectiveness, cost comparisons with other treatment options, and cost savings to the health system), patient/parent acceptability, patient/parent preference, patient experience (e.g., convenience, comfort, satisfaction, and trust), and a comprehensive approach to feasibility (consent rate, completion rate, assessment completion rate, return rate for each session, extent/likelihood/manner in which an intervention is implemented as planned, practicality, adaptation opportunities, integration into other assessment or treatment protocols, potential expansion to other patient populations, and addressing limited efficacy testing including long-term outcomes, larger sample sizes, etc.).

Presently, further research is needed linking inclusion/exclusion criteria to effectiveness and utility of CHIRP, ways to minimize attrition, and more detailed program evaluation to address feasibility, cost, acceptability, and other indicators. Future directions for the CHIRP intervention should include transition of the CHIRP treatment to online or mHealth modalities that can engage tech-savvy adolescents.

Making CHIRP Work for You

Program Philosophy and Engagement

Importance of Interviewer Style and Strategy

Perhaps the most difficult concept to communicate in a treatment manual is the interpersonal style and demeanor that the clinician should adopt in working with particular patient populations. Many clinicians consider the patient population (and their parents) treated in CHIRP to be highly challenging in terms of creating significant clinical change. Some families can come to treatment highly defensive, requiring considerable tact and patience on the part of the clinician. It is critical for you to acknowledge and validate patient and parental distress and concerns while thoroughly reviewing previous evaluations and intervention experiences. This process also entails an exploration of the symptom-related anxieties and worries of the teen and family. It is important to avoid premature causal assumptions; that is, maintain a willingness to keep valid medical issues in mind and judiciously explore them without encouraging excessive or unnecessary diagnostic tests and treatment procedures. Furthermore, it is important to investigate such factors as timing, social/environmental context, and characteristics associated with symptom presentation and/or exacerbation.

The differential diagnosis of the patient's health problem should not be reduced to merely diagnosis by exclusion (i.e., elimination of readily demonstrable organic causes). Indeed, a premature dismissal of serious underlying physical disease may lead to misdiagnosis and treatment misadventures and failure. Rather, view assessment as an ongoing interpersonal process that is reassuring, validating, educating, rapport- and trust-building, and leading to a collaborative commitment to improve patient functioning.

Adopting a Rehabilitation Perspective

In adopting a rehabilitation perspective as opposed to a cure, youth and their families are encouraged to accept that their symptoms, including pain and/or fatigue, may or may not go away completely. Interventions are aimed at helping the patient and family move their focus away from total elimination of symptoms as a necessary condition for progress and toward improved functioning. An overemphasis on total elimination of symptoms is contraindicated because it prompts the teen to focus more attention on bodily sensations and increases perceived symptom intensity. In contrast, treatment emphasizes improving the patient's coping skills in order to increase daily functioning. Thus, improved adaptive functioning is employed both as the goal of treatment and as an index used to measure progress.

Importance of the Initial Session and Establishing Commitment

One crucial point cannot be overemphasized. The primary goal of the first encounter/session is to accomplish the following:

- Validate that the patient's illness and symptoms are real and not "in his or her head"; communicate to the adolescent and family that you "get it": you understand the illness and its impact on daily life.
- Acknowledge the varied and often frustrating experiences the patient and family have endured in their efforts to arrive at a diagnosis and get helpful guidance about addressing its impact on the teen's lifestyle. With some conditions this may even involve getting health care professionals and others to understand and believe in their condition and its impact on the adolescent and family.
- Instill a sense of hopefulness that the treatment approach has and can (in the patient's own situation) lead to gradual significant improvement in functioning.

This experience of validation begins to lay the relational foundation for engaging the patient and family in committing to taking an active role in the treatment process. Your task is to tactfully guide the teen and family from a relentless pursuit to finding a "cure" before addressing the teen's functioning, to a more multifaceted approach involving coping with symptoms, graduated improvements in functioning and quality of life, and appropriately altered expectations and lifestyle modifications. While reduction of some symptoms may occur in the course of treatment, it is not the primary emphasis of the intervention nor is it realistic with some health conditions.

Pediatric Pain and Fatigue in Coping with Chronic Illness

Recurrent and chronic pain is a common presenting concern in pediatrics, with estimated median prevalence rates for painful conditions ranging from 11% to 38% (King et al., 2011; Perquin et al., 2000). Pain can present in children as their primary concern (e.g., amplified musculoskeletal pain syndrome or complex regional pain syndrome) or may be among a constellation of symptoms in multifaceted chronic illnesses (e.g., pediatric cancers, IBD, juvenile idiopathic arthritis, or sickle cell anemia) (Law, Noel, Nagel, & Dahlquist, 2017).

Given the American Academy of Pediatrics' focus on the "opioid epidemic" (Eccleston & Clinch, 2007) and the dangers of dependence and even addiction for patients who are prescribed these medications, it is important that alternative treatments be made available. This may include nonopioid pharmacological options (antidepressants, acetaminophen, nonsteroidal antiinflammatory drugs [NSAIDs]), as well as nonpharmacological options not provided in CHIRP (e.g., massage, transcutaneous electrical nerve stimulation [TENS] units, acupuncture/acupressure, physical therapy, or sleep aids) and, for some patients with persistent severe debilitating pain, an interprofessional pain program in a day hospital or inpatient setting. This may be particularly important given the finding that patients with chronic pain are often high utilizers of costly health care services.

The CHIRP approach embraces a biopsychosocial conceptualization, common among investigators in the field of chronic illness and chronic pain, leading to a shift away from dualistic attempts to differentiate physical from mental or emotional pain, or "organic" versus "nonorganic." This model acknowledges the multidimensional nature of symptoms in which biological, psychological, individual, social, and environmental variables are bidirectional in the development, maintenance, and subjective experience of pain, fatigue, and disability (American Pain Society, 2001; Basch, Chow, Logan, Schechter, & Simons, 2015; Bursch, Joseph, & Zeltzer, 2003; Hyams & Hyman, 1998; Law et al., 2017; Valrie, Bromberg, Palermo, & Schanberg, 2013; Zelter, Bursch, & Walco, 1997; Zeltzer, Tsao, Bursch, & Myers, 2006). In the area of chronic pediatric pain, researchers have pointed to changes in the CNS, termed "central sensitization," to explain the effects that recurrent and chronic pain have on concentration, clarity of cognition (e.g., "brain fog"), fatigue, mood, and deconditioning, which is circularly connected to reduced activity (Bromberg, Schechter, Nurko, Zempsky, & Schanberg, 2014; Kashikar-Zuck et al., 2014; Rabbitts, Holley, Groenewald, & Palermo, 2016; Schmidt-Wilcke & Clauw, 2011; Wolfe, 2009; Wolfe, Hauser, Hassett, & Katz, 2011; Woolf, 2011). CNS changes are frustrating because they are experienced as stressful and further complicate coping efforts, thereby exacerbating pain symptoms; further causes for the centralized symptoms may not show up on traditional medical tests. As a result, many pediatric pain patients seeking mental health and integrated approaches have likely exhausted diagnostic workups and conventional medical treatments, and they often feel frustrated and hopeless. The CHIRP intervention can be of great benefit to these teens and their families in addressing pain and fatigue associated with chronic illness, whether it is the primary or secondary concern. A supplemental session (see Workbook, Chapter 11, The Problem of Chronic Pain) is provided to more specifically address the needs of teens for whom chronic pain is a significant factor in their health challenges.

A growing body of literature supports the efficacy of a CBT and of an ACT approach to treat chronic health conditions in youth (Abbott et al., 2017; Eccleston et al., 2014; Lewandowski, Palermo, Stinson, Handley, & Chambers, 2010). Components of these treatments, like relaxation training, have been associated with reductions in the frequency and intensity of symptoms including pain, headaches, distress, and improvement in functional impairment (Agoston & Sieberg, 2016). Similarly, learning to pace activity and improve sleep hygiene habits can positively impact chronic symptoms, resulting in a rippling positive effect on poor outcomes (Lewandowski, Palermo, De la Motte, & Fu, 2010).

Of course, CHIRP and/or an outpatient model may not be appropriate for all patients. When symptoms and functioning are too severely affected, an intensive program may be more suitable (see the American Pain Society statewide listing of programs at http://americanpainsociety.org/get-involved/shared-interest-groups/pediatric-adolescent-pain; see also Banez et al., 2014; Logan et al., 2012; Maynard, Amari, Wieczorek, Christensen, & Slifer, 2010; Weiss et al., 2013). The immersion into an intensive program can more powerfully increase functioning and physical activity, enhance coping, reverse harmful family dynamics, and jump-start the process of self-management of patient lifestyle and health condition (Hechler et al., 2014; Simons, Sieberg, Pielech, Conroy, & Logan, 2013). Upon return from an intensive program, adolescents and their families often will need guidance to enact skills taught during their stay. Skilled therapy using CHIRP and its requisite skills can be invaluable to reinforce the skills taught, especially in tailoring their use in day-to-day implementation at home.

Family Factors

Many researchers and clinicians involved in the study and treatment of complex pediatric health conditions have endorsed a stress appraisal and coping model in which child disability and family disruption are a function of the child and family interpretation of symptoms, type of coping employed (problem-focused or emotion-focused), and parental attempts to support the child's efforts to cope (Folkman, Lazarus, Gruen, & DeLongis, 1986; Lipani & Walker, 2005; Zeltzer et al., 2006). Other recent studies suggest that, in some families, some of the child's symptoms, particularly pain and fatigue, may play a functional role within family interaction patterns and relationships. In these families, functional disability may be more a result of these interaction patterns than of the subjective experience of symptoms (Covelman, Scott, Buchaanan, & Ross, 1990; Kopp et al., 1995; Logan & Scharff, 2005; Naidoo & Pillay, 1994; Scharff et al., 2005). Undeniably, such symptoms as chronic pain and fatigue have an adverse impact on the overall quality of life for both the adolescent and the family (Hunfeld et al., 2001).

In studies that have examined the social consequences of chronic illness in children, more solicitous parental responses have been associated with greater sick role behavior and greater functional disability independent of stress level or pain intensity (Gidron, McGrath, & Goodday, 1995; Van Slyke & Walker, 2006; Walker, Claar, & Garber, 2002; Walker, Garber, & Greene, 1993; Walker & Zeman, 1992; Whitehead et al., 1994). For example, caregivers' expressions of sympathy, attention to symptoms, emotional reactions, modeling of symptoms, and reinforcement of sick role behaviors by allowing escape/avoidance of responsibilities all have been associated with greater disability in children (Fordyce, 1976; Garber, Zeman, & Walker, 1990; Liakoupoulou-Kairis et al., 2002; Payne & Norfleet, 1986; Schanberg et al., 2001).

A study of children with chronic functional abdominal pain experimentally manipulated whether parents attended to or distracted the child from symptom complaints during visceral discomfort induced by a water load provocation task. When parents attended to symptom complaints, their children exhibited nearly twice as many such complaints (Walker et al., 2006). Other studies examining the relationship among anxiety, depression, and chronic pain have found that more depressed and anxious children tend to have more functional disability compared to children with similar pain who are less emotionally distressed (Kashikar-Zuck et al., 2001; Palermo, 2000; Peterson & Palermo, 2004). Furthermore, there is evidence that, regardless of the perceived pain severity, when children regard their pain to be a serious health-threatening condition and their coping ability to be low, their pain tolerance is lower.

In CHIRP, you should be on the lookout for family dynamics that may have preceded and/or evolved around the patient's symptoms and may impede patient independence and optimal functioning in the course of treatment. These dynamics may include the following:

- *Overprotection/enmeshment.* This reflects the tendency of family to restrict the adolescent's activities in the service of recovery, which may in fact reinforce inactivity and contribute to deconditioning. In extreme situations, this may involve the parent(s) excessive contact, involvement, and even overidentification with the teen.
- *Misguided support.* In their efforts to support the patient, family members may engage in behaviors that undermine the teen's

confidence and sense of independence. This may involve either lowering expectations or applying excessive pressure for rapid change and improvement in function.

- *Communication pattern.* Family communication patterns may involve poor conflict resolution, difficulty communicating affect, and avoidance of discussing emotionally charged issues.
- *Attributions.* Patient and family may tend to attribute both illness and recovery to factors outside themselves and often beyond their control (i.e., an external locus of control).
- *Patient independence in managing illness.* Patient self-confidence is often undermined via immersion in the ill role, whereby family members increasingly take over the teen's responsibilities and provide assistance that may not necessarily be needed (closely related to overprotection/enmeshment and misguided support).
- *Social/peer dynamics.* Patients with chronic, complex medical conditions can become anxious and avoidant of normal peer situations after long periods of isolation away from school and social events. Look for patterns of social avoidance and lack of confidence in social interactions.

Coping, Cognitive Style, and Personality Factors

For adolescents suffering from chronic illness that interferes markedly with daily functioning, the level at which they are able to function is influenced by a number of individual and systemic factors including child and family interpretation of the teen's symptoms, type of coping employed, and parental attempts to support their child's efforts to cope with their symptoms (Folkman et al., 1986; Lipani & Walker, 2005; Zeltzer et al., 2006). Studies have repeatedly shown that many children who are coping poorly with their chronic health condition are characterized as having too few and ineffective coping strategies and perceive themselves as having a lack of control over many aspects of their symptoms (Branson & Craig, 1988; Dunn-Geier, McGrath, Rourke, Latter, & D'Astous, 1986). Claar, Walker, and Smith (1999) found that increased functional disability was more strongly related to self-report of lower levels of perceived competence (academic, social, and athletic), suggesting that functional disability may be reinforced if it allows avoidance of activities in which the teen believes themselves to be ineffective or unsuccessful. Additionally, Claar et al. (1999) observed that chronically ill youth with increased functional disability exhibited a tendency toward perfectionism and setting exceedingly high expectations. When teens employ more active coping strategies, they tend to have a greater sense of control and display less functional disability, less social withdrawal, and fewer complaints of pain (Flor, Birbaumer, & Turk, 1990; Siegel & Smith, 1989).

With regard to symptoms of persistent pain, adolescent patients have been observed to report greater pain behavior if they exhibit a cognitive pattern of "catastrophizing." This concept refers to the extent to which a person focuses on pain and makes exaggerated and fearful appraisals of pain symptoms and their consequences while regarding themselves as lacking the capacity to successfully cope. This cognitive style appears to be associated with increased pain severity, lower pain tolerance, greater functional disability, more anxiety and depression, and increased use of analgesics (Crombez et al., 2003; Vervoort, Goubert, Eccleston, Bijttebier, & Crombez, 2006). The presence of learning disabilities, unrealistic goals in a high-achieving perfectionistic teen, early pain experiences, a passive or dependent coping style, marital problems in the home, and chronic illness in a parent have all been shown to be associated with increased functional disability (Hyman et al., 2002). These individuals often express strong beliefs that medical professionals will provide a passive unitary medical solution to their condition (medication, surgery, etc.) and, in response, take little personal responsibility for managing their symptoms or lifestyle behaviors contributing to their disability. Typically, these patients' primary coping strategy is to decrease activity and involvement when they experience symptoms.

Bursch and colleagues (2003) propose a model whereby disability associated with symptoms develops when a physical trauma, illness, or other life circumstance becomes overwhelming to a vulnerable teen who has poor coping skills and cannot regulate their own distress. Furthermore, the physical symptoms may allow the teen to avoid or escape the stressor, associated discomfort, and negative emotions. Consequently, they may develop a behavior pattern in which avoidance of stressful/painful stimulation and subsequent failure to develop positive coping strategies compound each other, thereby increasing dependence on others, social withdrawal, avoidance of school and social and physical activity, leading to a progression of functional disability.

Clinically, we and other investigators (Garralda, 1996) have found patients experiencing significant functional disability with their chronic illness to manifest some of the following qualities worthy of clinical attention:

- Extreme conscientiousness, obsessiveness, sensitivity, and insecurity
- Anxious with a tendency to set high standards of achievement resulting in placing considerable stress on themselves
- Family members who may overtly or covertly tend to impose high academic and behavioral standards

Fidelity with Flexibility

In employing a manualized intervention such as CHIRP, it is important for the clinician to strive to achieve fidelity to the program model while also having the flexibility to accommodate unique patient and family needs. While manualized treatment programs like CHIRP provide a strategy for the structure and sequencing of therapeutic activities, they cannot replace your judgment in any individual patient, family, or group encounter. CHIRP has been designed to allow you to select an intervention that targets the primary concerns of the patient as they arise in therapy. For example, a patient in Session 3 repeatedly brings up the topic of her difficulties with wanting to please others, which leads her to avoid expressing her own needs and at times being taken advantage of by her peers. It becomes obvious to her clinician that it would be more effective to introduce the Assertiveness activities from the Teen and Family Workbook at this point, even though this intervention is not scheduled to be introduced until a later session. Mastering these interpersonal skills earlier in treatment becomes an important foundation for this patient's processing of other treatment activities and managing stress more effectively.

However, in the absence of a clear reason to deviate from the structure of the program, we recommend that you follow the sessions as presented in the CHIRP Clinician Guide. This may be particularly true when employing CHIRP in a group format (see Appendix I: CHIRP Group Intake Form and Appendix H: Conducting CHIRP in a Group Format). The sequencing of therapeutic activities has been based on a wealth of clinical experience with these patient populations and is designed to enhance the "joining" process while minimizing patient/family/group participant defensiveness early in treatment. Bottom line: employ a specific intervention out of sequence *if clinically indicated*, but do this at a minimum. The integrity of the CHIRP structure is important to conducting an effective treatment program.

Who Is Not an Appropriate Candidate for CHIRP

Not every patient with a chronic illness will benefit from the interventions employed in CHIRP. In particular, teens with developmental delay and significant communication problems may have trouble with the cognitive and communication emphases in the program. Patients with more severe psychopathology may lack the impulse control and emotion regulation skills needed to effectively participate in treatment activities. We have found that while children experiencing somatic concerns related to dissociative conditions (e.g., conversion disorders) benefit from many of the skills introduced in CHIRP, this is best preceded by more traditional individual and family psychotherapeutic and possibly psychopharmacological interventions. When employing CHIRP as a group intervention, it will be important to determine if the adolescent and/or parent/guardian exhibits personality characteristics that may be disruptive to the group process (e.g., poor emotional regulation and reactivity, demanding and domineering). Many teens will initially reject attending CHIRP in a group format due to their social anxiety and avoidance. However, it is our experience that these teens often blossom in the group intervention when given the opportunity to interact with other teens who are also facing the challenges of coping with a chronic illness.

Even when a patient and family are appropriate for CHIRP, your judicious application of other services or a referral may be needed. With a small proportion of patients, we have found the CHIRP interventions to provide a level of trust and relief that may open the door to the revelation of other, more deep-seated anxieties or trauma, including the effects of maltreatment and sexual abuse. It goes without saying that you must always be sensitive to the possibility of these factors being present in some patients. Additionally, individual psychotherapy may be needed for some associated issues such as comorbid anxiety, depression, obsessive-compulsive disorder, eating disorders, and social phobia, to mention a few.

Becoming Familiar with the CHIRP Materials

Assessment Measures

Use of Structured/Standardized Assessment Measures

Implementation of the CHIRP model is greatly enhanced by integration of assessment strategies to evaluate, inform, and guide treatment at all stages. A thorough initial evaluation provides specific information about target symptoms, history, background, family environment, and other domains of personality/behavior. Structured evaluation of target symptoms and important behavioral and psychosocial domains at the start of treatment provides a baseline for evaluation of change and effectiveness later in treatment. During treatment, regular structured evaluation can provide important information about progress and outcomes, which is used for feedback and modification of the program to flexibly respond to the needs of the teen and family.

Among the most helpful methods of assessment are questionnaires and behavior checklists. While the use of these standardized measures may be beneficial, it is critical to incorporate them into the broader context of evaluation and treatment to achieve the goals of CHIRP. For example, questionnaires and checklists should be used to augment, not substitute for, direct in vivo evaluation methods such as interviewing and behavioral observation. Additionally, the family's interpretation of and reaction to specific questionnaires and items should be considered. Overreliance on objective questionnaire assessment early in your contacts with the patient and their family may contribute to their perception that you believe their symptoms have a primarily psychological origin. Thus, measures should be chosen judiciously based on teen and family wariness or openness to discussion of the constructs that are targeted in the measures. Another consideration in the use of questionnaire or behavior checklist measures is the influence of the respondent on the results obtained from the measure. Factors such as rater bias, rater psychopathology, rater awareness of child behavior, and idiosyncratic rater interpretation of child behaviors can affect results in ways that may influence measure interpretation or compromise measure validity. You should familiarize yourself with the manuals and background research literature of the measures described in this section.

A large number of measures (predominantly questionnaires) exist to systematically assess and quantify symptoms, dynamics, and environmental characteristics related to child and family reaction to illness symptoms and sequelae. Appendix G: Suggested Assessment Measures, provides brief descriptions and citations for a large number of measures that are recommended as applicable for patients referred to CHIRP. In the following sections, we describe assessment strategies and instruments that may be used to structure and enhance implementation of the CHIRP model.

Structured Assessment Embedded in the CHIRP Evaluation Approach

Evaluation of child and family behaviors, symptoms, and characteristics at the start of a CHIRP intervention requires a general high-quality clinical evaluation with additional specific areas of assessment targeting illness-related adjustment and coping factors. Key components of the general initial clinical evaluation are summarized in Table I.1; suggestions for interview questions and questionnaire-based measures to assist in this general clinical evaluation can be found in Kronenberger and Meyer (2001).

In addition to a thorough basic clinical assessment at the start of CHIRP, specific measures are sensitive to the dynamics, reactions, symptoms, and adjustment of children presenting with significant illness symptoms. Use of these structured measures at the beginning and throughout the CHIRP intervention will provide quantitative information about patient status and progress in key areas of functioning. In addition to global domains important in reactions to illness, such as coping behaviors and family responses, specific symptom domains such as fatigue, pain, and sleep disturbance have broad and significant impacts on functioning and are therefore targeted for assessment across physical

Table I.1 CHIRP Evaluation Components: General Symptoms and Functioning

Respondent	Method	Broad domain	Specific areas of functioning
Parent	Interview/ Questionnaire	Review of symptoms	Presenting symptoms
			Other psychological symptoms
			Somatic symptoms
	Interview/ Questionnaire	History of present presenting symptoms	Presenting symptoms (history)
	Interview/ Questionnaire	Background and demographics	Family environment and history
			Medical history
			Social history
			Developmental history
			Academic history
			Family psychiatric history
Child	Interview/ Observation	Review of symptoms	Presenting symptoms
			Other psychological symptoms
			Somatic symptoms
	Interview/ Observation	Mental status and observations	Appearance
			Attitude
			Motor skills
			Thought processes
			Sensorium and intellect
			Thought content
			Sensation and perception
			Mood/Affect
			Speech-Language
			Self-concept
			Social skills and interaction
			Stresses and coping skills

(*continued*)

Table I.1 Continued

Respondent	Method	Broad domain	Specific areas of functioning
Teacher	Questionnaire	Behavioral and adaptive functioning	Behavior Assessment System for Children, Third Edition (BASC-3; Reynolds & Kamphaus, 2015) (We recommend reserving the use of the BASC only if there is a history of significant behavioral issues)

conditions. Table I.2 provides a summary of recommended domains of assessment and measures for evaluation of these domains. Appendix G: Suggested Assessment Measures, provides references and descriptions to all measures, as well as additional measures in the domains of interest.

Completion of all measures listed in Table I.2 is expected to take about 30 minutes total for parent and child. Most measures are brief (fewer than 30 items). These specific measures of illness-related symptoms and functioning should be administered at judicious intervals during the CHIRP intervention. The frequency of administration can be either flexible or planned, but evaluation using these measures at least once every 2 months is recommended.

Worksheets and CHIRP Forms

Information about CHIRP, including background, goals, descriptions of treatment components, and monitoring of progress, is facilitated by the use of several structured forms and questionnaires to monitor progress. The use of structured forms is recommended to improve treatment fidelity and structure, as well as to provide parents, patients, and referral sources with clear expectations and directions. Forms are found in the appendices to this Clinician Guide as well as within the CHIRP Teen and Family Workbook. A brief description of the forms in the appendices follows.

Table I.2 CHIRP Evaluation Components: Illness-Related Symptoms and Functioning

Broad domain	Respondent	Measure
Coping behaviors and skills	Parent	Child Observed Coping Scale (COCS)
	Child	KIDCope
Family response to child symptoms	Parent	Health Experiences and Behavior Inventory (HEBI)
	Child	Juvenile Health Experiences and Behavior Inventory (JHEBI)
Illness-related functional disability	Parent	Functional Disability Inventory—Parent Report (FDI-PR)
	Child	Functional Disability Inventory—Child Report (FDI-CR)
Life functioning (school, social, activities)	Parent	Barkley Functional Impairment Scale—Children and Adolescents—Parent Rating Scale (BFIS-CA)
Symptom ratings: Fatigue	Parent	Fatigue Severity Scale (FSS-P)
	Child	Fatigue Severity Scale (FSS)
Symptom ratings: Pain	Parent	Pediatric Quality of Life Pain Scale (PedsQL Pain Scale)
	Child	Pediatric Quality of Life Pain Scale (PedsQL Pain Scale)
Symptom ratings: Sleep	Parent	Pittsburgh Sleep Quality Index (PSQI)
	Child	Pittsburgh Sleep Quality Index (PSQI)

Appendix B: CHIRP Mastery Rating Scales

The use of the CHIRP Mastery Rating Scale (also called the Mastery Form) allows for the patient, parent, and clinician to survey and rate the extent to which the teen grasps and employs the skills that are taught in sessions and via homework assignments between sessions using the CHIRP Workbook. This form, which can be administered at each session or strategically throughout treatment, can also assist in tracking completion of all the skill areas addressed in the program. Ratings are made using the following scale (this is the teen first-person wording):

0 I do not understand this skill.
1 I understand this skill.
2 I practiced this skill in the CHIRP session (or group).
3 I used this skill outside of the CHIRP session (or group) at least once.
4 I used this skill on more than one occasion in an actual life situation.

Many of the skills taught in CHIRP will not be readily reflected in the ratings but likely will be observed in later sessions after the teen has had the opportunity to employ them. For example, if the patient completed the CHIRP Workbook activity on "Talking with Others About Your Illness" on May 15, then the clinician would give the teen a rating of 2 on the Mastery Rating Scale. Later in treatment, should the patient spontaneously report in a session that they approached their teacher about getting extended time (ideally from their 504 Plan) on a class project in order to avoid being overtaxed in their school work, which could worsen symptoms, then the clinician would record a 4 mastery rating to reflect the teen's spontaneous use of the skill in an actual life situation. You can download additional copies of the CHIRP Mastery Rating Scales form from the TreatmentsThatWork™ website at (www.oup.com/CHIRP).

Appendix C: CHIRP Program Brochure

This tri-fold brochure can be adapted for use in informing referring professionals about CHIRP. You can download additional copies of the brochure from the TreatmentsThatWork™ website at (www.oup.com/CHIRP).

Appendix D: CHIRP Physician Referral Form

This form can be provided to referring professionals to be employed in making a patient referral to the CHIRP clinician. Appropriate releases of information should be attached, along with summary clinical information from the patient's medical record. The form and supporting documents can be faxed, emailed, or sent via regular mail to the clinician. You can download additional copies of the CHIRP Physician Referral Form from the TreatmentsThatWork™ website at (www.oup.com/CHIRP).

Appendix E: CHIRP Interdisciplinary Communication Form

This form is employed in providing information to members of the interdisciplinary treatment team. Space is provided for including the fax numbers of all treating clinicians to maximize the likelihood that this information will be shared among them to ensure coordination and clear communication. Referring professionals get a "thumbnail" view of the CHIRP activities on this form, thus further educating them about the treatment approach while monitoring the patient's progress through treatment. Within the context of the 12-session model, this should ideally be done at the beginning of treatment and every 3 to 4 sessions to update all treating clinicians on patient/family progress and adherence. You can download additional copies of the CHIRP Interdisciplinary Communication Form from the TreatmentsThatWork™ website at www.oup.com/CHIRP.

Appendix F: CHIRP Feedback Form

This form is for use by the CHIRP clinician in communicating the initial assessment and treatment planning with the referring physician and other involved professionals. However, it is appropriate for use at other times during the treatment process. You can download additional copies of the CHIRP Feedback Form from the TreatmentsThatWork™ website at www.oup.com/CHIRP.

Appendix G: Suggested Assessment Measures

These measures, while most often used for research purposes, have clinical utility for assessing pain, fatigue, and functioning, as well adjustment, coping, attributional, and family factors. You can download additional copies of these suggestions from the TreatmentsThatWork™ website at www.oup.com/CHIRP.

Appendix H: Conducting CHIRP in a Group Format

There are a number of benefits to conducting CHIRP with teens in a group format, including reducing the social isolation experienced by many adolescents with chronic medical conditions. This supplement provides principles and guidelines for selecting patients and adapting CHIRP for group administration, including conducting a parallel group for parents of chronically ill teens.

CHIRP Session-by-Session

General Guidelines

The CHIRP treatment program has been developed to expose the patient and their parent(s)/guardian(s) to a series of exercises and activities that improve awareness of the interaction between illness and symptoms, enhance stress awareness and coping skills, and facilitate increased patient functional independence in management of recovery, problem solving, and decision making. The recommended session format is based on our extensive clinical experience in working with pediatric patients with a wide variety of fatiguing and painful illnesses and conditions. This is intended to be a suggested format, and you should always be aware of the need for flexibility in responding to unique individual patient and family needs.

Additionally, we caution you not to rely too readily on patient or parent assurance that the teen has already mastered all the information and skills covered in a particular module or activity. It is our experience that many of the adolescents suffering from chronic painful and fatiguing conditions place a premium on depicting themselves as highly competent and may minimize difficulties in any area of personal functioning. However, in the course of working on the activities in the CHIRP Workbook with the teen, it often will become apparent that, despite their initial assertions to the contrary, they are in obvious need of assistance with skill development in that area.

The use of the CHIRP Mastery Form (see Appendix B) will assist in ensuring that all activities and modules are covered in the course of treatment. Thus, by utilizing the CHIRP Session-by-Session sequencing as a general guideline and filling out the CHIRP Mastery Form, you can maintain flexibility and responsiveness to patient and family needs while at the same time documenting completion of the skill areas addressed in the program.

Reassurance/Anxiety Reduction

At the outset of treatment, patients and families can benefit from validation of their concerns and general reassurance that performing the activities in the CHIRP Teen and Family Workbook, along with close medical management and other therapies, will eventually lead to improved functioning and quality of life. Depending on the teen's medical condition, some symptoms may persist anywhere from months to years. However, active involvement in CHIRP will likely hasten improvement in coping and mood while enhancing overall functioning and quality of life. Additionally, we have found it valuable to employ patient stories, testimonials (we use video recordings of patients and families who have given their written permission), and anecdotal reports describing patient experiences in treatment associated with favorable, as well as unfavorable, outcomes.

Many patients referred to CHIRP have been diagnosed with conditions that are complex and medically less well-defined or delineated, such as fibromyalgia, CFS, and functional abdominal pain. These patients have often had negative experiences with health care providers and others in getting their disorders diagnosed and treated. Particularly for these adolescents and their families, we have found that the following guidelines for providing reassurance and positive treatment expectations are valuable early in the course of treatment. The accompanying scripts are intended to help you articulate the guideline to the patient and their family, and they should be reworded by you to suit your own style and the developmental level and communication style of the patient.

Guideline

In cases where the patient's condition has a generally favorable prognosis for symptom reduction (dependent on underlying medical illness):

Your doctors have run numerous tests to rule out serious illnesses (such as lupus, cancer, diabetes, etc.). While your symptoms have had a major impact on your life, fortunately we have good reason to believe that you are very likely to improve considerably and return to a more normal lifestyle.

Some patients may challenge this assurance by noting that they have suffered for several months (or even years) with their symptoms and have seen numerous doctors and specialists, yet they have experienced little or no improvement in symptoms. Additionally, other practitioners may have told the teen that *their* treatment approach would definitely help them, yet it was not beneficial. The patient may rightfully question why they should believe that their experiences in CHIRP would be any different.

I understand how you may be doubtful at this time. Many patients have been treated in the past as if they were exaggerating or making up their symptoms. Others tell us that this has led to a lack of trust and not feeling understood. I wouldn't blame you for feeling this way, given your experiences. Our approach recognizes that the symptoms of your illness affect all aspects of your life. In order for you to get better, we will need to take a team approach and work together with your doctors, specialists, therapists, and school staff to try to address the ways your condition affects your life. Together with your family, we will work on a set of activities that have helped others in your situation to get back to a more normal way of life. The change you are looking for will not happen without effort, nor will it happen overnight, but it can happen if we actively work on it together.

Guideline

Graduated exercise and activity, rather than inactivity and refraining from exercise, are important to facilitate recovery and improved functioning.

It is a natural tendency when we become ill to reduce or withdraw from our normal activities. In the case of short-term, minor illness, that's "just what the doctor ordered" and is important for your recovery. However, when a condition becomes chronic, and you refrain from engaging in your normal activities for an extended period, many people lose confidence and withdraw. This can lead to the worsening of symptoms. Some people may become more sensitive and reactive to stress. When this happens, you can become less able to tolerate activities that you used to handle just fine.

Guideline

Open communication (about feelings, thoughts, family interactions, barriers, fears, etc.) between all involved in the patient's treatment is of paramount importance.

Your treatment is a team effort between you, your family, me, and your other health care professionals. It is based on a relationship in which we all feel free to express our concerns, opinions, needs, and feelings about various issues that affect you, your illness, and the process of getting better. The truth is that you are the expert on "you," and we can only guide you through this process. In order for that to happen, we will need you to express your feelings about your experience of the things we are doing in this program. Then we can address issues as they come up and make your treatment fit your specific needs. This will make it much more helpful than if we blindly applied our approach to you as if you were not a unique individual.

Guideline

Emphasize the low probability of the patient developing other serious illness dependent on the underlying medical illness. This addresses "catastrophic thinking" when the teen and/or family are hesitant to participate for fear that the child might have an undiagnosed illness that would be made worse by increased activity; this guideline should only be employed when there is medical certainty that the teen does not have a serious or life-threatening condition that would be made worse by participation in CHIRP.

We do know that patients with your condition seldom go on to develop a more serious illness. We also know that your mood, beliefs, and attitude can have a bearing on your physical condition. For example, if you motivate yourself to stay physically active, this can affect your body's ability to heal itself by improving your ability to fight off disease and handle stress more effectively.

Rehabilitation Works (There Is No Magic Bullet!)

We have found it important throughout the course of treatment to communicate, in word and action, the following rationale for the rehabilitation-based intervention approach employed in CHIRP:

- An emphasis is placed on countering the effects of inactivity and de-conditioning via increased regular physical activity and exercise. This can be facilitated by active involvement in specialized physical and occupational therapy and graduated exercise.
- It is important to continually reframe the goal of treatment from finding a "cure" to coping with and overcoming the impact of the adolescent's symptoms and lifestyle on their life.
- Responsibility for managing most aspects of improved functioning is gradually shifted from you and the parents to the teen.
- Your role gradually moves to a more supportive and encouraging one.
- The treatment approach discourages the belief that the patient can safely return to normal developmental functioning *only* after symptoms have fully resolved.
- The teen is empowered as an active agent in treatment, with the goal of overcoming a challenging but manageable problem.
- Symptomatic improvement, however minimal, is a source of pride and is equated with personal success based on individual determination and hard work.
- An active problem-focused coping approach is needed to reduce symptom burden and improve functional impairment; it is important to discourage mere passive acceptance of the condition, which may lead to more inactivity.
- Academic accommodation and performance receive key emphasis. School attendance and performance are seen as indicators of functional improvement.

- A key therapeutic task is to manage patient and family anxiety and challenge perceptions of the teen as vulnerable and unable to cope.
- It is important for you to manage parental ambivalence and guilt over enforcing compliance with treatment objectives.
- Parents are encouraged to be both supportive and firm in a way that communicates to the teen that they are capable and competent to overcome their stress.
- Promote resilience! The rehabilitation approach challenges the perception of the patient as being highly vulnerable. This is a crucial foundation of a cognitive behavioral strategy emphasizing the child's fundamental health, strength, and adaptability.

Compliance with Homework in the CHIRP Workbook

A major challenge in any treatment endeavor, and particularly in participation-heavy manualized treatment programs such as CHIRP, is what to do when patients repeatedly fail to complete and bring in their assigned between-sessions homework. Another scenario is when the patient completes the written homework entries in the car on the way to the session or even in the waiting room before the appointment. If this happens only on rare occasions, it is best for you to tactfully remind the patient (and parent/guardian) that the activities of the treatment program are most helpful when the patient applies them regularly and to real-life situations as they arise between sessions. Many people with chronic illness have lost confidence in their abilities and need encouragement and reinforcement that change is possible with commitment and action.

However, when the patient fails to complete homework on a regular basis, particularly in the first few sessions, it suggests a deeper problem with motivation and readiness for or commitment to change. In such situations, the application of motivational interviewing strategies (Prochaska & DiClemente, 2005) and clarification of values may help the patient in participating more actively, to a point at which they experience improvement in their feelings and their functioning.

This may be enough to improve their adherence to homework assignments. However, there are always those patients whose state of readiness to change is in what Prochaska and DiClemente (2005) term the "pre-contemplation" phase. These patients should be treated nonjudgmentally, with an "open door" policy to allow them to return for treatment when they are ready.

Prep Session

Goals of the Session

- Introduce the treatment model and rationale.
- Establish rapport with the teen and family.
- Gather important evaluative information.
- Establish commitment to the outlined course of treatment.
- Develop a weekly program of physical activity.
- Discuss 504 Plan accommodations and school advocacy.

Introduce the CHIRP Treatment Model and Rationale

Committing to an active treatment program such as CHIRP can seem daunting to the patient and family for a number of reasons. First, many families have been through a rather protracted process in arriving at a diagnosis, including contacts with health care professionals who may have been doubtful about the veracity of the adolescent's illness. Additionally, the patient may have lost confidence in their ability to carry out expected daily activities such as attending school, participating in extracurricular activities, and maintaining active involvement with their peers. Understandably, the patient and family may be quite skeptical of any treatment approach that they consider "psychological" in nature to address symptom relief and recovery. Therefore, it is essential to help the teen and family understand the role of the structured activities in the CHIRP Teen and Family Workbook in facilitating recovery and returning to more normal functioning. The Introduction and Prep Session in the CHIRP Workbook has been carefully worded to communicate these principles in a palatable format, and you should review this section with the patient and family in the session. It helps for you to have reviewed this material before the session so that you can present this material in a more conversational fashion, rather than merely reading from the CHIRP Workbook.

Establish Rapport with the Teen and Family

The importance of establishing a relationship and obtaining a "buy in" by the patient and family cannot be overemphasized. To accomplish this, we suggest that you work toward the following:

- Validate that the patient's illness and symptoms are real and *not* "in his or her head."
- Acknowledge the varied and often frustrating experiences the patient and family have endured in their efforts to arrive at a diagnosis (e.g., getting health care professionals and others to understand and believe in their condition) and the patients/parents wanting a "fix" and not having found a clear explanation, unitary cause, and treatment.
- Instill a sense of hopefulness that the CHIRP treatment approach has, and can (in the patient's own personal situation), lead to gradual improvement in functioning.

This experience of validation begins to lay the relational foundation for engaging the teen and family in committing to taking an active role in the treatment process. Hopefully, you are able to tactfully redirect the patient and family from a relentless pursuit of a unitary "cure" to a more multifaceted approach involving coping with symptoms, graduated improvements in functioning and quality of life, and appropriately altered expectations and lifestyle modifications.

Establish Commitment to CHIRP

Clinical outcomes for teens and their parent(s) are highly favorable for those who complete all of the sessions in the CHIRP Teen and Family Workbook. Establishing such commitment from busy families can be a challenge. We have found it useful to formalize this process with a CHIRP Commitment Form (Appendix L), whereby the CHIRP clinician, the teen, and their parent(s)/guardian all sign the form at the beginning of treatment to affirm their mutual commitment to the collaborative process involved in the treatment program. While no formal data collection has been conducted to assess the effectiveness of this process, early experience with the use of this form in conducting CHIRP in teen group format has been encouraging.

Discuss 504 Plan Accommodations and School Advocacy

In addition, it is important to address school concerns as this is typically a major area of disruption in the lives of most children with chronic painful and debilitating conditions. Assess both the impact of patient illness on school attendance/performance (compared to premorbid functioning) and begin to address a graduated return to school with appropriate accommodations designed to minimize the impact of their symptoms on achievement. Having you serve as an advocate and liaison with the school facilitates patient and family validation and paves the way for the teen to become more active in treatment. Be prepared to provide the family with an appropriate letter, ideally by Session 2, to facilitate accommodations at school.

Assigning Homework

As determined to be necessary based on previous response to homework assignment, have the teen and parent(s) complete the following homework assignments and bring to the next session:

- Read "Introduction to CHIRP: Children's Health and Illness Recovery Program" in the Introduction and PREP Session of the Workbook.
- Read "Let's Get Physical" in the Introduction and Prep Session of the Workbook.
- Carry out your Weekly Activity and Exercise Action Plan (Worksheet I.1).
- Read "Considerations for School" in the Introduction and Prep Session of the Workbook.

After the Prep Session, if the family requests, you should prepare a letter advocating for 504 Plan school accommodations based on information gathered during the intake. This letter should ideally be given to the family by Session 2, or at least early enough in the treatment sessions to provide the teen with appropriate accommodations to meet their academic needs. You may need to take further steps, such as participating in phone conferences, if warranted, during treatment. Continue to check in with the family periodically about the use of these school accommodations and whether any changes need to be made. Sidebar I.1 provides an example of advocating for accommodations.

Sidebar I.1 Advocating for Accommodations

Jennifer, a 17-year-old with postural orthostatic tachycardia syndrome (POTS), has been on home-hospital instruction for more than 3 months after experiencing two episodes of syncope at school, where she fell to the floor and bruised her head. She was diagnosed with POTS by a pediatric neurologist, placed on antihypotensive treatments, and has recently started physical therapy. Upon starting CHIRP, it was advocated that a graduated resumption of school attendance be established. It was recommended to the school that Jennifer initially attend 1 hour of class per day, the first 2 weeks of her return to school. When this attendance was tolerated, then a gradual increase to two classes, a half-day, etc., was recommended every 2 weeks. Other accommodations involved providing a quiet testing environment, use of the elevator between classes, and extended time on tests and projects. Brief education of school staff on the nature of POTS, symptoms, and how they impact school and social functioning was conducted, along with an emphasis on the importance of a graduated approach to maximizing a successful return to a full-day school schedule.

Schools vary widely in their willingness and ability to make such accommodations, although they may be mandated under a 504 Plan. Under this provision, while the curriculum is not altered, teachers and administrators must provide instructional and environmental accommodations for the student pertinent to the disability associated with their health condition.

CHAPTER 1 Session 1: Stress Identification and Management

Session Format

Meet separately with parent(s) and teen.

> **Clinician Note**
>
> *Throughout the course of the Children's Health and Illness Recovery Program (CHIRP) intervention, it is important for you to meet separately with the parent(s) to address questions that have arisen between sessions, to obtain parental perspective on various aspects of the treatment model, and to more informally introduce concepts that will be developed further in the course of the sessions and that are geared toward encouraging more patient functional independence. It is up to your clinical judgment as to when during the session (beginning, middle, or end) and for how long these encounters are needed to maximize the impact of CHIRP interventions.*

Goals of the Session

- Review homework with the aim of identifying areas of difficulty, emerging themes, and progress based on completion of logs and monitoring of forms assigned at the last session. This includes Worksheet I.1: Weekly Activity and Exercise Plan.
- Introduce "Stress Identification and Management."
- Introduce the "Sleep Hygiene Guidelines."
- Instruct in the completion of Worksheet 1.3: Sleep Log.

Introduce Stress Identification and Management

Stress is universally present in nearly everyone's life. This can be particularly true for teens coping with a chronic health condition. As such, the topic of stress is a logical starting point for treatment. This topic evokes opportunities for the validation of the patient's experiences during the course of their illness and recovery process. Activities are designed to increase teen and family awareness of illness-specific and non–illness-specific stressors and their impact on the patient and their symptoms and to introduce general concepts of problem- and emotion-focused coping.

The concept of stress is perhaps the least threatening and conceptually the friendliest way to introduce the mind–body connection. In the presence of a chronic medical condition, the teen's sensitivity to stress may be heightened. A bidirectional relationship between stress and symptoms develops wherein the complications associated with a health condition add stress to the teen's life, while stressors unrelated to the illness (conflict with peers, striving for independence from parents, etc.) can further exacerbate their symptoms.

Begin by defining stress, with a clear emphasis on both "good" and "bad" aspects of the stress response. In this discussion it is important to help the teen identify the link between stress and physical cues in their body. Together you and the patient review the "Stress Identification and Management" material in the Workbook and complete Worksheet 1.1: List of Teen Stressors (see Sidebar 1.1 later in this chapter and Figure 1.1). The goal of this activity is to sensitize the patient to the fact that daily life is full of potential sources of stress, both illness-related and non–illness-related, which may impact physical functioning, symptoms, and emotional well-being. This discussion provides a building block for introducing a wide variety of related topics, such as coping strategies, relaxation, distraction, and interpersonal communication skills. Reviewing the List of Teen Stressors worksheet with the teen provides a less threatening format for getting the patient to talk about stress and "normalizes" that stress is a universal experience, particularly for patients with a protracted illness. The goal is to ascertain what stresses are most difficult for the patient in order to help them identify and manage these stressors more effectively, under your guidance and coaching. Of course, the adolescent may present with stressors that are not included in the list, and these can be added as needed.

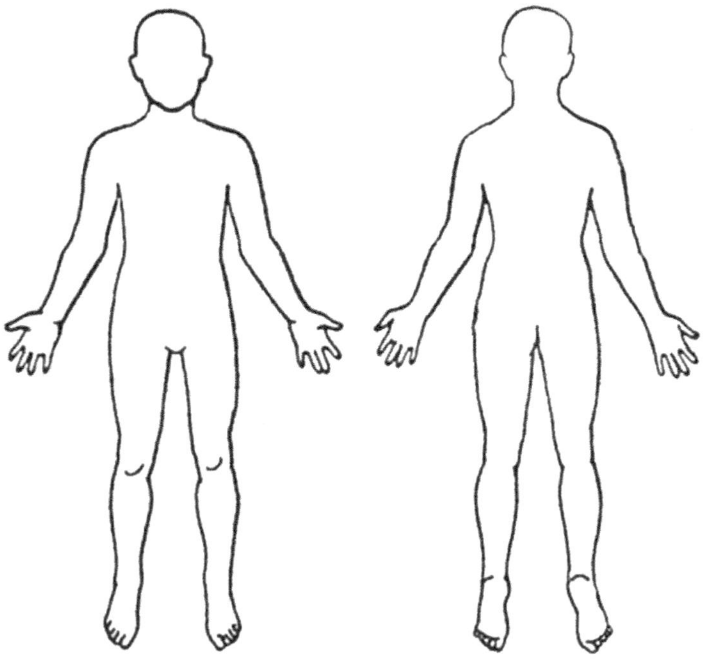

Figure 1.1
Stress and your body.

The teen should monitor their stress over the next week using Worksheet 1.2: Monitoring Your Stress. This involves their identifying four stressful situations and rating the intensity on a 1 to 10 scale. It will be helpful to work with the teen to define anchor points at the extremes and midpoints to establish variability based on their personal experience.

Sleep Activities and Hygiene

Most patients with chronic illness present with significant sleep disturbance, including difficulty falling asleep, shifts in sleep cycle (e.g., falling asleep at 3 or 4 AM and not awakening until noon or later), or disrupted sleep due to pain or discomfort. For this reason, it is important to introduce basic sleep hygiene guidelines early on in treatment to address sleep issues. Review the "Sleep Problems and Sleep Hygiene" material in the Workbook in session with the teen.

Sleep Log data (see Worksheet 1.3: Sleep Log) are to be kept for several weeks as you help the patient and parent(s) to identify factors contributing to sleep disruption and design interventions to modify sleep hygiene practices. This change is typically gradual, and interventions may be met with some resistance early in treatment. This may take the form of the teen complaining that sleep difficulties are beyond their control. However, careful monitoring via the Sleep Log and detailed questioning often reveal practices that actively contribute to sleep difficulties (e.g., staying on the computer or cell phone into the early morning hours). As you explore the patient's sleep patterns in more detail, be on the lookout for more serious sleep difficulties that may require referral (e.g., apnea, breathing-related sleep disorders). A blank copy of Worksheet 1.3: Sleep Log appears in Session 1 of the Teen and Family Workbook. For additional copies of this log, go to the TreatmentsThatWork™ website at www.oup.com/CHIRP.

Finally, you should work with the teen in reviewing and modifying their Worksheet 1.1: Weekly Activity and Exercise Action Plan. Many teens will either overdue or underdo physical activity scheduling, so you need to assist them in developing a more realistic graduated program of physical activity and exercise to which they are more likely to adhere.

Additional Clinician Activities

After Session 1, complete the CHIRP Interdisciplinary Communication Form (Appendix E) and send it to the identified members of the multidisciplinary treatment team. (You can download additional copies of this form from the TreatmentsThatWork™ website at www.oup.com/CHIRP.) Sending this form initiates the establishment of the multidisciplinary treatment team process. It is helpful to obtain fax numbers (and possibly email addresses) for all members of the team (e.g., referring physician, primary care physician, physical therapist, nutritionist, specialists) to be placed on the form so that each team member can fax information from their contacts to all members of the team. It is recommended that this form be updated and faxed after Sessions 4, 8, and 12. Of course, appropriate patient and guardian consent must be obtained.

Assigning Homework

As determined to be necessary based on previous response to homework assignment, have the teen and parent(s) complete the following homework assignments and bring to the next session:

- Read "Stress Identification and Management" from Session 1 of the Workbook.
- Complete Worksheet 1.2: Monitoring Your Stress for four situations.
- Read "Sleep Problems and Sleep Hygiene" from Session 1 of the Workbook.
- Complete Worksheet 1.3: Sleep Log.
- Refine/Implement Worksheet I.1: Activity and Exercise Action Plan.

Sidebar 1.1 Teen Stressors

Dan is a 17-year-old who had been diagnosed with asthma at age 14 and chronic mononucleosis about 3 months prior. While he had learned to manage his asthma fairly well by premedicating with rescue inhalers before vigorous physical activities, the level of fatigue and exhaustion he has experienced with mono has been almost more than he could bear. His school attendance has been plagued by frequent absences for several days at a time, and he has fallen behind in most of his subjects. The prospect of repeating algebra and history in summer school in order to officially start the school year as a senior has further discouraged him.

When Dan and his clinician reviewed the List of Teen Stressors worksheet, it seemed noteworthy that he had placed question marks in the boxes next to several items having to do with peer acceptance and relationships. When questioned, Dan initially brushed this off, chalking it up to the frequent and lengthy absences from school secondary to his mono infection. However, with further inquiry, Dan admitted that he was feeling increasingly isolated and cut off from the experiences his peers were having. When he did get together with some friends, his fatigue made it hard for him to join in with enthusiasm, and he often would make up an excuse to leave the activity early to come home and go to bed. Also, with his illness, Dan had lost weight, and he felt physically out of shape due to his inactivity. This made him more self-conscious around his peers and more avoidant.

Dan agreed to record his stress levels with the Monitoring Your Stress worksheet over the next week in order to monitor his response to various stressful situations at school, when out with friends, and at home. In reviewing his information, it became apparent that his increasing self-consciousness and associated avoidance of peer activities were major contributors to his feelings of isolation. In subsequent CHIRP sessions, interventions were targeted at facilitating Dan's gradual increase in his social contacts, working on his self-evaluations (Thought Changing) and communication and assertiveness skills with his peers.

CHAPTER 2 Session 2: Problem-Solving Skills

Session Format

Meet separately with parent(s) and teen.

Goals of the Session

- Review homework with the aim of identifying areas of difficulty, emerging themes, and progress based on completion of logs and monitoring forms assigned at the last session.
- Introduce "Controlling Stress Through Coping."
- Introduce "Solving the Problem" Coping.

Introduce Controlling Stress Through Coping

Briefly introduce the patient to the concept of "coping," with an emphasis on actively managing stress since stress can never be totally avoided and is a part of everyday life. Follow this discussion by differentiating between the two types of coping. We have labeled these "Solving the Problem" coping and "Managing the Impact" coping, to use terminology more familiar and descriptive for patients and families. You may be more familiar with the constructs of *emotion-focused coping* and *problem-focused coping*. The focus of Session 2 will be primarily on understanding and employing problem-solving skills. However, it is important to work with the teen to identify when each type of coping is most likely to be effective. It may be helpful to frame this discussion around what aspects of the situation the teen is and is not able to control. Figure 2.1 in the CHIRP Workbook will be particularly helpful in conducting this discussion.

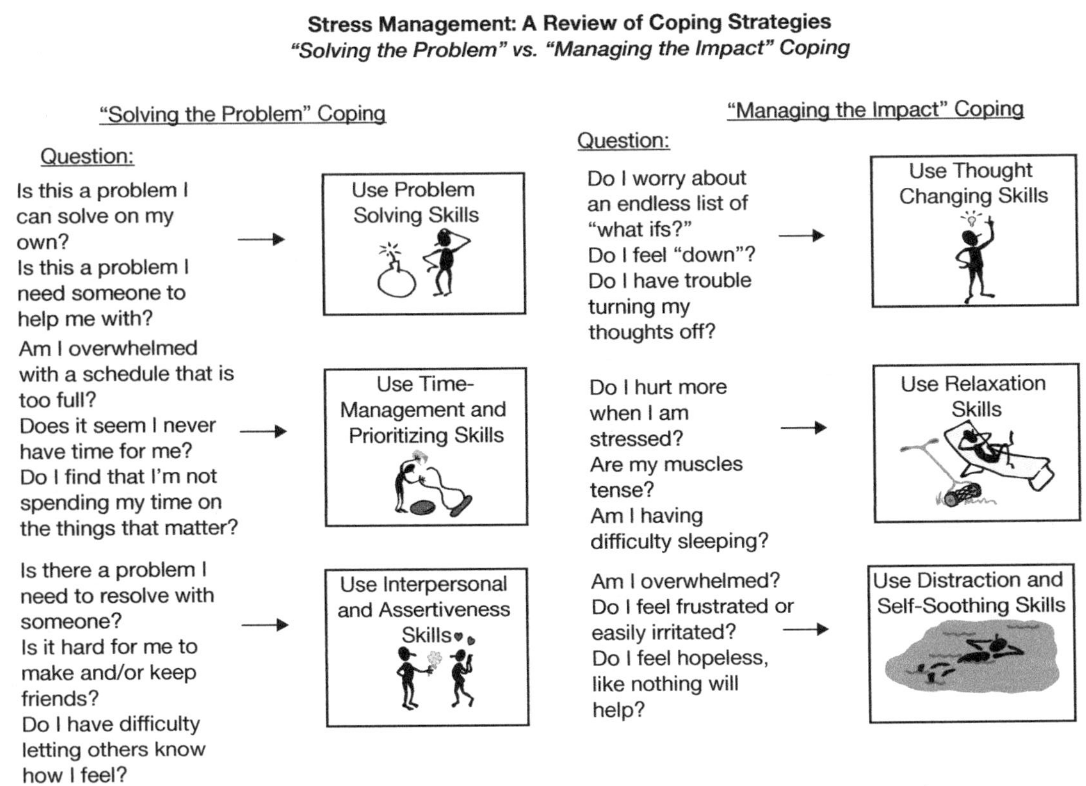

Figure 2.1

Stress management: a review of coping strategies.

Introduce "Solving the Problem" Coping

Interventions focused on helping teens and their parents to improve active problem-solving skills have been frequently employed in assisting patients with chronic illness, pain, and emotional difficulties such as depression and anxiety. The activities in this session are designed to provide teens with the more adaptive coping skills needed to actively confront problems, as opposed to ignoring or avoiding them. These include experiences in learning how to identify clearly defined problems, brainstorming multiple solutions, evaluating the pros and cons of proposed solutions, and developing a flexible action strategy.

In your session with the teen, use of the worksheets will facilitate their beginning to understand and master the specific steps of problem solving, starting with Worksheet 2.1: My Biggest Concerns List. Encourage the teen to identify up to five primary problems or concerns they are experiencing currently. Then, have the teen select one of the problems from the list and, employing Worksheet 2.2: Brainstorming Solutions, work with them in generating several potential solutions to the identified problem. Don't be afraid to generate some whimsical solutions to help the teen become more flexible in their generation of potential solutions. Particularly high-achieving and perfectionistic adolescents can often be quite rigid and restrictive in considering potential problem solutions. Using Worksheet 2.3: Possible Solutions, have them explore the pluses and minuses of each generated solution and then rank order the solutions according to their potential effectiveness. The last step is to transform the preferred solution into a detailed action plan using Worksheet 2.4: Your Action Plans. This procedure is employed repeatedly throughout the Children's Health and Illness Recovery Program (CHIRP) sessions, reinforcing a more systematic approach to problem solving as a key coping and stress management strategy. Using Worksheet 2.5: How Well Did Your Plan Work?, the teen will then complete Step 5 as homework, focusing on evaluating the outcome of their problem-solving plan. Sidebar 2.1 shows an example of the application of problem-solving strategies to improve sleep-related difficulties.

Finally, before ending the session, review the teen's Sleep Log (Worksheet 1.3) and Weekly Activity and Exercise Action Plan (Worksheet I.1) and provide them with new worksheets for the coming week. (For additional copies of these worksheets, go to the TreatmentsThatWork™ website at www.oup.com/CHIRP.) Addressing sleep and physical activity will be an ongoing focus while the teen and family are in CHIRP.

Assigning Homework

As determined to be necessary based on previous response to homework assignment, have the teen and parent(s) complete the following homework assignments and bring them to the next session:

- Complete Problem-Solving Coping Step 5 (Worksheet 2.5).
- Continue filling out Worksheet 1.3: Sleep Log.
- Refine/Implement Worksheet I.1: Activity and Exercise Action Plan.

Sidebar 2.1 Improving Sleep-Related Difficulties

Lanette is a 14-year-old girl diagnosed with juvenile fibromyalgia whose symptoms have resulted in considerable impairment in multiple areas of her life including school attendance, athletic involvement, peer relationships, and social activities. She attended several appointments with different specialists over a period of months before being diagnosed and admittedly had grown much more dependent on her mother who also suffered from an extensive medical history and who accompanied Lanette to most of her appointments. It was difficult for the mother to see her daughter upset, so the mother gradually began to step in and minimize the demands and stress placed on the teen. Lanette was not required to do as much around the house, and her mother began to take on responsibilities that Lanette used to be able to face on her own.

During one session with her CHIRP clinician, Lanette brought up her increasing difficulties with getting herself awake, up, and out of the bed in the morning. Her mother had assumed the role of being an alarm clock, going into her room and attempting to wake her up over a period of several hours during the morning. At this point, Lanette shared that the task of waking herself up seemed impossible. It was apparent to the clinician that the teen had become dependent on her mother to get her up, and her mother had become part of the problem by not imposing consequences for her daughter oversleeping. A vicious and ineffective cycle had been established.

Lanette and her CHIRP clinician identified the problem in the following terms:

Problem: *Lanette is unable to wake up because she continually pushes the snooze button on her smartphone alarm.*

The CHIRP clinician assisted Lanette in brainstorming multiple potential solutions to the problem. These included the following: don't go to school at all or at least go on home-hospital/home-bound schooling to avoid the stressful demands of the morning routine; have her mother start the process of waking her up earlier (e.g., start at 5 instead of 7 AM); schedule her least favorite class for first period so that she could go to school late and avoid attending the class; set her own alarm to wake up on her own; establish a more reasonable bedtime routine so Lanette would be less tired in the morning; and buy a physical alarm clock with no snooze button and place it in a location across the room, requiring her to get out of bed to shut it off. It is important to note that the clinician was willing to consider both positive and negative solutions in the brainstorming process.

After reviewing the pros and cons to each of these proposed solutions, Lanette decided on a plan for establishing a regular bedtime routine and, if that did not work, purchasing a regular alarm clock. Lanette and her mother agreed to work on the bedtime routine first, with the new alarm clock solution as a backup. To address potential barriers to these solutions (Lanette was admittedly not particularly motivated to attend school), she and her mother incorporated a contingency plan to hold Lanette more accountable (getting a hot breakfast if she got up on her own; loss of privilege of using social media for the day if she did not get up on her own; taking public transportation if she missed the school bus, etc.). Over the course of several weeks, Lanette and her mother were able to identify barriers to implementing the plan and, with their clinician, were able to adjust these strategies to maximize Lanette being more personally accountable for getting herself up and ready for school.

CHAPTER 3 Session 3: Relaxation Skills

Session Format

Meet separately with parent(s) and teen.

Goals of the Session

- Review homework with the aim of identifying areas of difficulty, emerging themes, and progress based on completion of logs and monitoring forms assigned at the last session.
- Introduce "Managing the Impact" Coping.
- Teach Relaxation Skill I: Diaphragmatic Breathing (DB).
- Teach Relaxation Skill II: Progressive Muscle Relaxation (PMR).
- Introduce "Thought-Changing Skills."

Introduce "Managing the Impact" Coping

The goal of this instruction is to provide the teen with skills needed to manage the impact that their symptoms and other stressors have on their daily life, even if they cannot immediately be changed or resolved. Teens learn to cope with illness-related stressors as well as general stressors that, if overwhelming, may exacerbate symptoms. Specific strategies taught and practiced over a series of sessions include progressive muscle relaxation, diaphragmatic breathing, guided imagery, thought-changing skills, and "acceptance." These activities are often supplemented with such strategies as mindfulness meditation training, clinical biofeedback, etc. The patient and parents are coached in adopting these skills as lifestyle practices rather than as merely "techniques" to employ when symptomatic. The considerable body of evidence supporting the efficacy of these interventions is emphasized throughout treatment as these may be unfamiliar to patients and require considerable coaching and correction to employ habitually and effectively.

Teach Relaxation Skills I (DB) and II (PMR)

Instruct the patient in relaxation skills involving DB and PMR. It is important to take time to actually instruct the adolescent in these skills so that they can accurately practice them between sessions. It can also be helpful to supplement these activities with aids such as viewing a video demonstration, providing a recorded relaxation script, using simple biofeedback equipment or strategies to make the relaxation more concrete, and modifying the environment to provide a more relaxing atmosphere (soothing music, dim lighting, recorded nature sounds such as ocean waves or a quiet stream, use of comfortable chair, etc.). Emphasis should be placed on daily practice (typically at least 20 minutes daily) in order to promote generalization of these skills beyond the context of the therapy session. There are also a number of useful smartphone applications that can facilitate this process. Additionally, patients should keep a simple log of their practice (refer to Worksheet 3.3: Relaxation Skills Practice Log in the Workbook) to monitor their progress and establish a link between the use of these strategies and overall reduction of stress.

Introduce Thought-Challenging and Thought-Changing Skills

For many patients, the connections between thoughts, feelings, and behavior are not clear. Worksheet 3.1: How Thoughts and Images Affect Our Emotions provides an exercise that you can employ in your session with the teen that illustrates how our thoughts/beliefs and the images we generate can drive the emotional and behavioral responses we have to life experiences.

As the Children's Health and Illness Recovery Program (CHIRP) clinician, it is your job to facilitate a better understanding of the bidirectional relationships between thoughts, emotional responses, and behavioral responses in general and in particular as they pertain to the patient's physical symptoms. Figure 3.1 in the Workbook demonstrates this relationship. As you are introducing the Thought Record homework to the teen (Worksheet 3.2: Thought Record), help the teen differentiate between thoughts, feelings, and actions. For example, in social situations, patients may report feeling "stupid" when they are actually *feeling* anxious based on the *thought* that others view them as behaving in an odd or unacceptable way. Often patients struggle with identifying the thoughts driving their reactions. This struggle provides an opportunity for you to help the teen articulate underlying beliefs that may lead to their affective reactions while also providing you with an understanding of the teen's level of insight into the thought-feeling-behavior connection. For instance, a teen who reports thinking, "I don't like this" when encountering a group of peers at the mall may need help extending this statement to "I don't like feeling like this! I feel like an outsider, a misfit. I just don't seem to fit in with them anymore." Such a statement reveals both the potential cognitive distortions ("Since I haven't hung out with them for weeks, I'll have *nothing* to talk about and will feel out

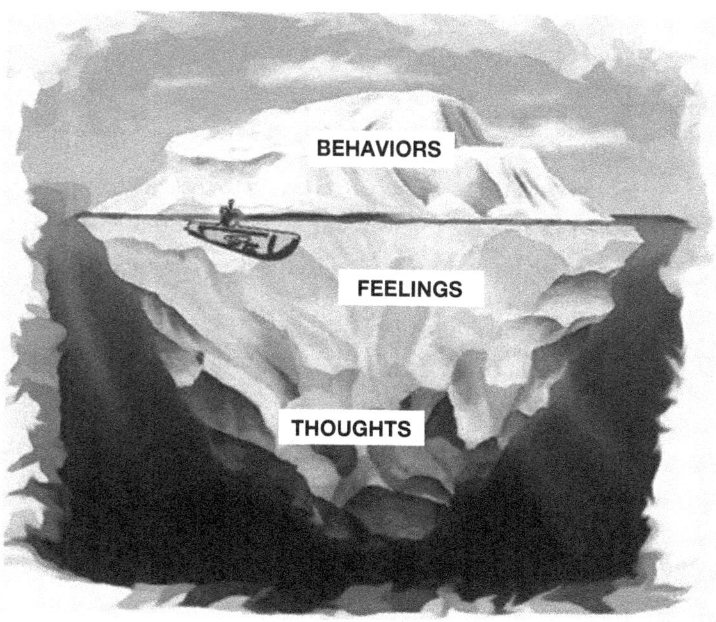

Figure 3.1
Thought iceberg.

of place") and the lack of understanding of the thought-feeling-behavior connection.

The patient is instructed on how to fill out a Thought Record and given homework (Worksheet 3.2) to complete before the next session, without filling in the Alternative Thoughts column, which will be explained in the next session. They should record information from at least three situations between sessions. Sidebar 3.1 shows an example of using cognitive behavioral therapy (CBT)-based skills to identify distorted automatic thoughts and subsequently engage in thought-challenging and thought-changing skills in addressing social anxiety often experienced by teens with chronic illness who have had periods of social isolation related to their health condition.

Finally, before ending the session, you should review the teen's Sleep Log (Worksheet 1.3) and Weekly Activity and Exercise Action Plan (Worksheet I.1) and provide them with new worksheets for the coming week. (For additional copies of these worksheets, go to the TreatmentsThatWork™ website at www.oup.com/CHIRP.) Remember, addressing sleep and physical activity are an ongoing focus while the teen and family are in CHIRP.

Assigning Homework

As determined to be necessary based on previous response to homework assignment, have the teen and parent(s) complete the following homework assignments and bring to the next session:

- Continue filling out Worksheet 1.3: Sleep Log.
- Work on Worksheet 3.2: Thought Record. Record information from at least three situations.
- Start filling out Worksheet 3.3: Relaxation Skills Practice Log.
- Refine/Implement Worksheet I.1: Activity and Exercise Action Plan.

Sidebar 3.1 CBT Skills in Addressing Social Anxiety

Jamie is a 15-year-old preparing for his family vacation. His parents have encouraged him to invite a friend from school to accompany them, but Jamie is hesitant to do so. In session, he states that he would feel pressure to entertain his friend during the entire vacation, and he does not want to have a "high-maintenance" trip. When examining Jamie's thoughts and feelings about inviting his friend, his Thought Record reveals feelings of nervousness associated with thoughts of responsibility for his friend's happiness and enjoyment. Jamie believes his friend will find him boring and difficult to have fun with and predicts his friend will not want to go on any subsequent trips with Jamie's family or hang out with him in the future.

(*Continued in Session 4.*)

CHAPTER 4 Session 4: Thought-Challenging and Thought-Changing Skills

Session Format

Meet separately with parent(s) and teen.

Goals of the Session

- Review homework with the aim of identifying areas of difficulty, emerging themes, and progress based on completion of logs and monitoring forms assigned at the last session.
- Review and reinforce "Challenging Your Automatic Thoughts."
- Together work on practice Worksheet 4.1: Challenging Your Thoughts.
- Introduce "Acceptance and Coping."

Introduce Thought-Challenging Skills

Discuss Worksheet 3.2: Thought Record, which the teen completed as homework from Session 3, emphasizing the identification of negative automatic thoughts contributing to distress in the example situations. Using the "Challenging Your Automatic Thoughts" material in this session of the Workbook, engage the teen in a discussion of common cognitive errors (e.g., hopelessness, catastrophizing, perfectionism). These errors highlight negative thought patterns related and unrelated to their chronic health issues and contribute to their distress, thus exacerbating their physical and psychological symptoms. For some patients, their illness may interfere with their ability to achieve the goals they had for themselves prior to illness onset. For others, the psychological impact of their symptoms (loss of confidence, pessimistic world view, external locus of control, etc.) may interfere with their willingness to set challenging yet appropriate goals for themselves. Feelings of inadequacy may be amplified, resulting in an overarching maladaptive schema that maintains functional disability, which interferes with the attainment of crucial adolescent developmental mastery experiences. As the clinician, remember that, for many highly anxious patients, the exploration and subsequent disclosure of their private thoughts of inadequacy and anxiety can be difficult.

In order to challenge these maladaptive cognitions, work with the teen using Worksheet 4.1: Challenging Your Thoughts. The teen is asked to weigh the evidence in support of or in opposition to their automatic thoughts. Based on evidence generated, the patient is then guided in developing an alternative, reality-based thought, which can be transferred from the Challenging Your Thoughts worksheet to Worksheet 4.2: Thought Record with Challenges. Using the final column of the Thought Record, help the teen reflect on how the newly generated Alternative Thoughts affect the quality and intensity of their affective response.

Introduce Acceptance and Coping

In dealing with chronic illness, the teen is faced with situations over which they have very little control. While the Children's Health and Illness Recovery Program (CHIRP) aims to enhance teens' ability to control their overall well-being, there are situations where significant distress cannot fully be avoided. In these situations, it is important that the teen cultivates a willingness to accept what cannot be changed and learns to employ coping strategies that minimize suffering, even when a situation is painful and distressing. This involves you assisting the patient (and family) in focusing on finding meaning in even the most challenging of experiences. In Worksheet 4.3: Practice Sheet for Developing Alternative Thoughts, sentence stems are provided to guide the patient in developing thoughts that are consistent with an acceptance-based approach to coping (e.g., "My illness has made my life harder at times, and as a result of these challenges I am stronger; more tolerant of distress; and I have developed wisdom, gratitude, and a new appreciation of life in my struggle"). Increasing acceptance of symptoms and perseverance despite limitations are often positive predictors of improved functioning. While a detailed explanation of more involved clinical strategies such as acceptance and commitment therapy (ACT; Hayes, Strosahl, & Wilson, 1999) is not possible here, many principles from this evidence-based approach are applicable to the treatment of patients with chronic, painful, and fatiguing conditions.

The challenge to the clinician working with teens with chronic illness is getting them to realize that most situations are not an either/or dichotomy. Of particular importance is the notion that physical symptoms and functioning are not mutually exclusive. One can be in pain while still engaging in meaningful pursuits. This is the ultimate way of empowering our patients. Life is no longer contingent on the quality or severity of symptoms.

Finally, before ending the session you should review the teen's Sleep Log (Worksheet 1.3), Weekly Activity and Exercise Action Plan (Worksheet I.1), and Relaxation Skills Practice (Worksheet 3.3) and provide them with new worksheets for the coming week. (For additional copies of these worksheets, go to the TreatmentsThatWork™ website at www.oup.com/CHIRP.) Remember, addressing sleep and physical activity are an ongoing focus while the teen and family are in CHIRP.

Assigning Homework

As determined to be necessary based on previous response to homework assignment, have the teen and parent(s) complete the following homework assignments and bring to the next session:

- Continue filling out Worksheet 1.3: Sleep Log.
- Begin to work on Worksheet 4.2: Thought Record with Challenges.
- Continue filling out Worksheet 3.3: Relaxation Skills Practice Log.
- Refine/Implement Worksheet I.1: Activity and Exercise Action Plan.

Sidebar 4.1 Thought-Changing Skills in Addressing Social Anxiety

(*Continued from Sidebar 3.1*)

Employing thought-challenging strategies, Jamie and his clinician went on to identify specific cognitive errors (i.e., mind reading, fortune telling) which the teen will then be able to challenge in order to develop more adaptive alternatives, i.e., engaging in thought changing. As he explores the evidence supporting and refuting his beliefs, Jamie is able to develop a more realistic appraisal of the situation. His challenging alternative thought was, "It doesn't make sense for me to worry that my friend won't enjoy being on vacation with me. After all, it was his decision to join me, and we have enjoyed spending time together in the past. All I can do is try to enjoy myself and the good company." In identifying and challenging the distorted thoughts/beliefs underlying his self-consciousness while also continuing to seek out this relationship, Jamie makes an important step toward thought-changing in overcoming unrealistic expectations of himself.

CHAPTER 5 Session 5: Time Management and Prioritization

Session Format

Meet separately with the teen and bring parents into the session during discussion of time management and scheduling.

Goals of the Session

- Review homework with the aim of identifying areas of difficulty, emerging themes, and progress based on completion of logs and monitoring forms assigned at the last session.
- Teach Imagery Skills.
- Teach "Time Management and Prioritizing" (and complete Steps 1 and 2 as described later in this chapter).

Imagery Skills

In addition to the diaphragmatic breathing and progressive muscle relaxation skills the teen has been taught, for some individuals the use of guided imagery is valuable in helping them achieve a deeper relaxation state and a better understanding of the mind–body relationship. For example, creating an image of holding a warm mug of hot chocolate while sitting by a fire indoors on a cold snowy winter day may be accompanied by a corresponding increase in hand temperature. When initiating guided imagery, you should begin by prompting the teen to generate a scene in which they feel secure, comfortable, and calm. This is facilitated by the use of Worksheet 5.1: Your Relaxing Scene in the Workbook. Be sure to guide the teen in incorporating and engaging multiple senses in order to create a deeper sense of relaxation. One helpful image that benefits patients with chronic pain involves seeing themselves free of pain and discomfort. For at-home practice it may be helpful to provide the teen with a recording of the instructions and accompanying imagery script made by you or even in the adolescent's own voice.

Teach Time Management and Prioritizing (Steps 1 and 2)

Many teens with chronic illness are either under- or overscheduled in their activities. For some, the teen may have unrealistic and even perfectionistic high expectations for what they can achieve in a given day, resulting in feeling overextended and increasing their level of stress. Many of these teens are unwilling to give themselves permission to take a short break, accept help from others, or refrain from taking on too much. In other cases, the teen has adopted an inactive, sedentary, and withdrawn approach to living their day-to-day lives that reflects an avoidant adaptation that often contributes to a depressed mood and further reduces their level of motivation to participate in activities that promote improved functioning (i.e., a sense of connection to others, enjoyment, and mastery). In either case it is important for you to help the teen distinguish between desired (want to) and required (have to) activities. This is facilitated by having the teen complete Worksheet 5.2: Your List of "Want to's" and "Have to's." Many teens (and parents) have difficulty with this distinction, particularly those who are perfectionistic or high-achieving.

After working with the teen on Worksheet 5.2 to help them better delineate their "Want to's" and "Have to's," it is helpful to meet with the teen and the parent(s) conjointly to apply this in clarifying responsibilities at home and developing appropriate and reasonable expectations for both the teen and parent(s) regarding the teen's daily functioning. When teen and parent disagree on necessary activities, the opportunity may arise to examine communication skills and conflict resolution.

Next, incorporating information obtained in the conjoint meeting with the teen and parent(s), you will work individually with the teen in filling out Worksheet 5.3: Weekly Schedule, as accurately as possible to reflect the teen's "Want to's" and "Have to's" identified in Step 1. In constructing their weekly schedule, you may notice ways that the teen is overscheduled or underscheduled (i.e., reflecting inactivity). This will provide the opportunity, using Worksheet 5.4: Your *Prioritized* "Want to's" and "Have to's," to revise their list employing more realistic or reality-based criteria. Employing Steps 3 (Prioritize), 4 (Remove, Revise, and Rewrite), and 5 (Evaluate Your New Schedule), the teen's homework then will be to put this schedule into action and begin prioritizing and revising the schedule, using Worksheet 5.5: Weekly Schedule Revised, in response to identified challenges, barriers, the observed imbalance between their "Want to's' and "Have to's," and feedback from their parents and others. Ideally, the teen's Weekly Schedule form will be revised several times over the course of the Children's Health and Illness Recovery Program (CHIRP) intervention as they and their parent(s) become more aware of the importance of prioritizing in response to the teen's physical condition and functioning.

Overall, it is important for you to assist the patient and parent(s) in understanding the complex relationships between symptoms, functioning, and activity scheduling.

Finally, before ending the session, review the teen's Sleep Log (Worksheet 1.3), Weekly Activity and Exercise Action Plan (Worksheet I.1), Thought Record with Challenges (Worksheet 4.2), and Relaxation Skills Practice Log (Worksheet 3.3) and provide them with new worksheets for the coming week. (For additional copies of these worksheets, go to the TreatmentsThatWork™ website at www.oup.com/CHIRP.) However, it is important to be clinically sensitive and not overwhelm the teen with too many worksheets at one time. Use your judgment in prioritizing which worksheets are the most valuable for the teen at any given point in treatment with CHIRP.

Assigning Homework

As determined to be necessary based on previous response to homework assignment, have the teen and parent(s) complete the following homework assignments and bring to the next session:

- Continue to develop Worksheet 5.1: Your Relaxing Scene.
- Complete Steps 3, 4, and 5 and the corresponding worksheets in the "Time Management and Prioritizing" section in this session.

- Continue filling out Worksheet 1.3: Sleep Log.
- Continue filling out Worksheet 4.2: Thought Record with Challenges.
- Continue filling out Worksheet 3.3: Relaxation Skills Practice Log.
- Refine/Implement Worksheet I.1: Activity and Exercise Action Plan.

Sidebar 5.1 Time Management and Prioritization Skills

Paige is a 14-year-old girl who came to CHIRP due to chronic health concerns with persistent pain and fatigue associated with her diagnoses of chronic fatigue syndrome, juvenile fibromyalgia, hypermobility syndrome, persistent headaches, and gastrointestinal symptoms. Prior to her diagnoses she had been very active in dance and, despite her pain and fatigue, continued her participation on two competitive dance teams. Her dance practices often resulted in Paige starting her homework late in the evening, thus pushing her bedtime to almost midnight on many occasions. Being a very achievement-oriented teen, Paige was reluctant to give up any of her current activities despite the adverse impact on her symptoms.

In her group CHIRP session focusing on prioritizing and time management, Shawna, another teen in the group, commented on Paige's Weekly Schedule, which was virtually full: little to no down time and a sleep schedule that averaged less than 6 hours of uninterrupted sleep a night on weeknights. When Shawna shared how improving her own sleep hygiene was having a positive impact on her symptoms and energy level, Paige asked her to help her revise her own schedule to make more time for sleep and free time. The next day, Paige made the decision to drop one of her competitive dance teams; 3 weeks later, in the teen group, she reported a significant improvement in her lifestyle and symptoms.

CHAPTER 6 Session 6: Increasing Teen Independence

Session Format

Family-Focused Session 1: Since Session 6 and subsequent sessions in the Children's Health and Illness Recovery Program (CHIRP) focus increasingly on interpersonal relationships and parent–teen dynamics, certain sessions will be tagged as "Family-Focused Sessions." While previously the teen and their parent(s) may have been seen together for part of a session to address various topics (e.g., scheduling), in Family-Focused Sessions the preferred format is to work conjointly with the teen and parent(s) for all, or at least most, of the session. This format is necessary both for you to observe the ways the teen and parent(s) approach such issues as problem solving and decision making, as well as to provide them with coaching and feedback in developing more effective communication strategies that can help increase teen confidence and skills in becoming more independent in managing their lifestyle.

Goals of the Session

- Review homework with the aim of identifying areas of difficulty, emerging themes, and progress based on completion of logs and monitoring forms assigned at the last session.
- Emphasize the importance of empowering the teen to become more independent in managing their illness and returning to more normal functioning.
- Explore teen and parent views of typical teen lifestyle.
- Assess the impact of symptoms on teen functioning.

Review Time Management Steps 3–5

Review Worksheet 5.5: Weekly Schedule Revised with the teen and parent(s). In particular, it is important to assess if this revised schedule is more realistic in keeping with their level of functioning and stage of recovery. Many teens continue to overschedule themselves and have difficulty establishing a balance in their need for rest, sleep, exercise and recreation, socializing, and studying. When feeling better, they may be prone to overdoing it, which may be followed by symptom exacerbation and a dramatic decline in functioning.

Some patients have coped with their illness through severely decreased activities and may have had to go on home-hospital/home-bound services rather than attend school. It is important for these patients, who may experience lowered feelings of self-confidence academically and socially, to not underschedule themselves. These teens and their parent(s) may need considerable support in planning and scheduling new activities that they may feel unsure of trying.

Increasing Teen Independence

After reviewing homework, with both the patient and parent(s) in the room together, introduce the concept of independent functioning. This should be approached in as nonthreatening a manner as possible. Many patients and their parents, after having to deal with the disruptive effects of the adolescent's illness on their independence, feel conflicted over just how much independence to expect from the teen. The forced dependence associated with the debilitating effects of the patient's symptoms can gradually undermine both teen and parent confidence in the teen's ability to engage in even minimal day-to-day activities. The parent(s), in their efforts to be "helpful," may inadvertently assume roles and responsibilities that the adolescent handled readily before becoming ill, which further undermines the teen's sense of self-efficacy. This is often a subtle process, but one that must be addressed to empower and engage the teen in the recovery process.

While these difficulties should be characterized as natural in the course of recovery, you should work with both teen and parents to understand how this dynamic can become unhelpful in the context of important normative developmental experiences. Invite the family to discuss how their interactions and lifestyle have been altered in response to the illness with the aim of raising the family's awareness of changes that may have occurred over time. Restricted activity outside the home is a common theme, yet more subtle changes may be discovered, such as increased parental control or teen minimization of the impact that the symptoms have had on daily life. While some alteration in family interaction is necessary, family members' attempts to accommodate the teen's symptoms often interfere with the natural course of development and leave loved ones feeling as though they are "walking on eggshells."

Over time, efforts to assist the teen may transform into tendencies to underestimate their ability or desire to manage age-appropriate responsibilities, thus depriving the teen of critical mastery experiences. For example, issues as basic as removing teen responsibility for household chores, enforcing bedtime rules, managing their daily schedule, etc., can set up a scenario in which the teen, over time, has fewer opportunities to accumulate evidence of their ability to effectively manage life challenges and future stressors. Alternatively, some families may assume that their formerly high-achieving and perfectionistic teen has already mastered all the essential skills needed to transition to adult life and does not need the skills introduced in CHIRP.

Parental beliefs will begin to emerge during this discussion, and it is important to take note of those parental behaviors that interfere with the teen's independence. For example, many parents of chronically ill children hold the belief that, "There's no such thing as helping my child too much!" (This will be covered in the family discussion of "Misguided Support" in Session 8.) It is of critical importance that you help parents recognize the deleterious effects of protecting their child from every potential source of distress—whether physical or emotional in nature—under the assumption that avoiding these experiences is a necessary part of their child's recovery. Such overprotection is a direct contradiction of what has been learned about chronic illness coping and optimizing functioning.

This discussion provides an opportunity to help the family engage in active coping and problem solving, over time creating a model of how to respond to the challenges of a chronic illness in a way that does not undermine the teen's motivation and feelings of self-efficacy. Parents' own observations of the adolescent's attempts at lifestyle adjustments provide important information; however, at times you will need to intervene if parent–teen interactions become confrontational, demeaning, or otherwise unproductive. In this case, before proceeding, it may be necessary to discuss aspects of parent–teen communication and establish guidelines for discussions. Future sessions will provide more in-depth treatment of communication strategies. However, be prepared to establish a framework for more positive parent–teen interactions in session, with an emphasis on mutual respect, taking turns, active listening, and so on.

Explore Teen and Parent Views of Typical Teen Lifestyle

Next, using Worksheets 6.1: Typical Teen Weekly Schedule (Teen) and 6.2: Typical Teen Weekly Schedule (Parent), have the teen and parent(s) explore together their concepts of a typical activity schedule for a healthy teen. This exercise gives you important information about the family's expectations of baseline functioning. For example, some families tend to consider a schedule that would be overwhelming to many as "normal." Other families believe it necessary and reasonable to absolve the patient of manageable responsibilities in the service of recovery from illness, which may reinforce symptoms, undermine confidence, and further limit functioning. Therefore, it is helpful to sensitively explore areas where the teen may regain independence and to increase parents' awareness of how they may be undermining their teen's independent functioning. Throughout the entire course of treatment, the ongoing challenge is to help teens and parents avoid overidentification with the sick role and develop a more flexible view of functioning that strikes a more adaptive balance between reasonable accommodations and developmentally typical activity.

In further examining the family's perception of a normal schedule, it is important to investigate differences in expectations from weekdays to weekends. In particular, noting extreme shifts in sleep schedules may highlight an area for intervention. Additionally, this activity can serve as a prelude to future therapeutic work regarding family communication skills. While comparing teen and parent expectations, you may observe how they address differences in views. Often this session serves to provide both clinician and family with a more nuanced understanding of the role of family dynamics in the recovery process.

Assess the Impact of Symptoms on Teen Functioning

The next objective of this session is to assess the extent to which the teen's symptoms interfere with participation in developmentally typical life experiences. As homework, instruct the teen and parent(s) to complete Worksheet 6.3: Illness Impact on My Weekly Schedule (teen completes) and Worksheet 6.4: Illness Impact on My Teen's Weekly Schedule (parent completes), which are used to facilitate this exploration. It is important to achieve this goal in a nonthreatening manner. When instructing the family on this task, consider using terminology such as, "Where have your symptoms gotten in the way?" or "If you did not have [diagnosis], how would your day-to-day life be different?" This will help to assess the teen's baseline functioning with the goal of leading the teen and parent(s) into developing a more realistic appraisal of the adverse impact that their symptoms have had on their ability and motivation to live life to the fullest. Be sure to examine potential patterns of limitation, which may be suggestive of particular difficulties, such as social anxiety, phobias, school avoidance, learning difficulties, family conflict, and/or enmeshment stemming from parents' own psychological vulnerabilities. By identifying symptom interference across multiple domains of functioning, the teen and parent(s) are given a multidimensional view of functioning that reinforces gradual progress in their recovery.

In their assigned homework for this session, the teen and parent(s) are to jointly complete Worksheet 6.5: Brainstorming a More Normal Teen Schedule. This task enjoins teen *and* parent(s) in generating a variety of ways in which the teen can become more independent across multiple domains of functioning.

Near the end of Session 6, in the section "Avoid the Avoidance Cycle!" discuss with the teen (without the parent) the material and case example. Using a personal example from the teen, have them complete

Worksheet 6.6: Pros and Cons of Avoidance as homework before the next session. Avoidant coping strategies are frequently seen in teens who are functioning below their potential, and completing this worksheet places avoidance on the agenda in facilitating the teen's use of more adaptive coping strategies.

Finally, before ending the session you should review the teen's Sleep Log (Worksheet 1.3), Weekly Activity and Exercise Action Plan (Worksheet I.1), Thought Record with Challenges (Worksheet 4.2), and Relaxation Skills Practice Log (Worksheet 3.3) and provide them with new worksheets for the coming week. (For additional copies of these worksheets, go to the TreatmentsThatWork™ website at www.oup.com/CHIRP.) Remember, it is important to be clinically sensitive and not overwhelm the teen with too many worksheets at one time. Continue to use your clinical judgment in prioritizing which worksheets are the most valuable for the teen at any given point in treatment with CHIRP.

Assigning Homework

As determined to be necessary based on previous response to homework assignment, have the teen and parent(s) complete the following homework assignments and bring to the next session:

- Continue filling out Worksheet 1.3: Sleep Log.
- Continue filling out Worksheet 4.2: Thought Record with Challenges.
- Continue filling out Worksheet 3.3: Relaxation Skills Practice Log.
- Fill out Worksheet 6.3: Illness Impact on My Weekly Schedule (this assignment is for the teen).
- Fill out Worksheet 6.4: Illness Impact on My Teen's Weekly Schedule (this assignment is for the parent[s]).
- Complete Worksheet 6.5: Brainstorming a More Normal Teen Schedule (this assignment is for both teen and parent[s] together).
- Fill out Worksheet 6.6: Pros and Cons of Avoidance.
- Refine/Implement Worksheet I.1: Activity and Exercise Action Plan.

Sidebar 6.1 Empowering the Teen

During a family session, 18-year-old Joni reveals that she is depending greatly on family members to manage her illness. For example, her mother has to wake her in the morning or she will sleep through taking her morning medications. Her father notes that he will get Joni drinks throughout the day, fix routine meals, and collect her dirty laundry. Even Joni's 12-year-old sister has been answering Joni's cell phone and declining conversations for Joni when her friends call. In session, Joni's parents relate that they support Joni's plan to get her own apartment once her symptoms improve.

A system is then established whereby Joni is given the responsibility of taking her medications, and she chooses how she prefers her parents to "check-in" to make sure she is not having difficulty. In addition, Joni and her parents select a few household chores that Joni can complete, with the collective goal of promoting her independence and supporting her eventual goal of living away from home.

CHAPTER 7 Session 7: Assertiveness and Relationships

Session Format

Meet separately with parent(s) and teen.

Goals of the Session

- Review homework with the aim of identifying areas of difficulty, emerging themes, and progress based on completion of logs and monitoring forms assigned at the last session.
- Guide teen in socially getting back into the loop.
- Introduce "Assertiveness Skills: The Three R's."
- Introduce "Communicating with Assertiveness (Steps 1 and 2)."

Review the Pros and Cons of Avoidance

Take time to review the materials on the cycle of avoidance that were assigned for homework during the previous session (including Worksheet 6.6: Pros and Cons of Avoidance). Disability has been shown to develop when physical trauma, illness, or other life circumstances become overwhelming to a vulnerable child who has poor coping skills and cannot regulate their own distress. In the context of a chronic illness, the physical symptoms experienced by teens may allow them to avoid or escape stressors, associated discomfort, and negative emotions in general. This can result in a behavioral pattern in which sources of potential stress and discomfort are avoided altogether, subsequently resulting in failure to develop more active coping strategies. This vicious cycle ultimately leads to increasing dependence on others, social withdrawal, avoidance of school and physical activity, and progression of functional disability. After reviewing the "Avoiding the Avoidance Cycle" materials from Session 6 individually with the teen and then conjointly with the teen and their parent(s), take time to identify the costs and benefits (Worksheet 6.6: Pros and Cons of Avoidance) of coping via avoidance, with an emphasis on both short- and long-term outcomes of perpetuating avoidant behaviors.

Getting Back into the Loop

The content introduced in this session emphasizes the importance of communication and assertiveness in the process of recovery from chronic illness. When an illness becomes protracted, it becomes increasingly important that the teen develop ways of communicating with others about their symptoms and their ability to participate in normal adolescent activities to whatever extent is reasonable and with family members in determining personal responsibilities and independence.

Begin by exploring the teen's network of relationships using Worksheet 7.1: Relationship Map. Then discuss with the teen how their relationships have changed as a result of their symptoms, the major challenges in their current relationships, and social situations that create discomfort. Have the teen complete Worksheet 7.2: Your Relationship Challenges with you in the session. This can help highlight areas where the teen is struggling in their ability to initiate and maintain meaningful relationships. Throughout this discussion, focus on the importance of returning to normal social functioning, broadening the scope of their current relationships, and diversifying and expanding their network of social support. The skills introduced later in this session will be employed to overcome the identified social challenges and increase the teen's sense of confidence in getting back into the loop.

Introduce Assertiveness Skills: The Three R's

Frame the discussion of communication and expression of one's feelings in the context of the "Three R's of Assertiveness." Begin by defining assertiveness and differentiating this way of communicating from more passive or aggressive approaches. Assertiveness is conceptualized not as a special response to unique situations. Instead, assertiveness should be presented as a way of regularly interacting with others that more clearly and accurately communicates one's feelings, perspective, opinions, desires, and preferences. Once assertiveness has been defined and is clearly understood by the teen, introduce the concepts of requesting, refusing, and rebutting. It can be particularly helpful to elicit personal examples from the teen's life in which they were faced with each of these three tasks. Using Worksheet 7.3: Assertiveness Quiz take time to process how the teen handled the situations and their emotional responses (i.e., comfort vs. discomfort) with the experience.

Many teens, in the process of accommodating the life changes that come with a chronic illness, experience diminished confidence in communicating with others and being assertive in a variety of social contexts. This often leads to more passive ways of coping with stress and discomfort via avoidance as opposed to assertive communication. A common teen response to discussing assertive communication is their belief that being assertive is mean, rude, or "no matter what I say or how I say it, it won't make any difference and I might even offend the person I am talking to." It is important to be on the lookout for these beliefs as they readily undermine the teen's use of the strategies that are so crucial to improving their functioning and independence.

Introduce Communicating with Assertiveness (Steps 1 and 2)

In the process of the patient undergoing complex medical evaluations, parents often assume an increasingly active role in communicating with doctors and other health care providers. Under such conditions, it is easy for the teen to slip into a passive role, relying on parents to become the "experts" on their illness and treatment. Therefore, equipping the teen with assertiveness skills is paramount in promoting self-efficacy and empowerment in taking a more active role in the process of recovery.

Step 1 involves working with the teen to identify strengths and weaknesses in their assertive communication skills. Worksheet 7.4: Identifying Your Assertiveness Strengths and Weaknesses is a particularly helpful tool to identify patterns of strengths and weakness in assertive communication, such as general difficulty asserting needs or more situation-specific challenges (e.g., group vs. public settings, familiar vs. unfamiliar peers, peers vs. adults, and medical settings vs. school and community). For some teens, a particular issue in communication may be identifying and expressing feelings. Worksheet 7.4 provides space for the adolescent to insert additional situations from personal experience. This provides an opportunity for the Children's Health and Illness Recovery Program (CHIRP) clinician, teen, and parent(s) to explore the common illness-related scenarios that have presented a challenge for the teen and which could have benefitted from assertive communication (e.g., communicating with health care professionals about treatment; informing others of physical limitations; and requesting accommodations at school, work, and other settings).

In Step 2, you will introduce the assertiveness guidelines (Worksheet 7.5: Assertiveness Guidelines), taking the time to explain each strategy and elicit examples from the teen's personal experience to ensure a clear understanding. Next, prompt the teen to consider which strategies have been and/or may be most challenging in the future.

Step 3 (assigned homework) encourages the teen to begin putting assertiveness skills into actual practice. For many teens, this experience is helped by in-session practice employing clinician–teen role-plays to try out various statements while providing corrective feedback when the teen uses too passive or too aggressive communication strategies. In their homework, using Worksheet 7.6: Assertiveness Opportunities, the teen applies the assertiveness guidelines in their identified challenging situations and begins developing a script for communicating about their medical condition. Teens should use Worksheet 7.6 to track their progress over the next several weeks, beginning with the least threatening situations and progressing to those that elicit greater discomfort. This exercise will provide the teen with opportunities to gain confidence using assertive communication in increasingly challenging scenarios.

Worksheet 7.7: Talking with Others About Your Illness is also completed by the teen for homework, with the aim of facilitating assertive communication in the context of their medical condition. It is anticipated that the teen will become more competent in requesting, refusing, and rebutting, in turn leading to a greater sense of confidence and control and less reliance on more passive forms of coping, such as avoidance. It should be emphasized to the teen that while communicating assertively does not guarantee the teen's preferred outcome in various situations, it most certainly increases the odds of their feeling understood and getting their needs and desires met compared to either saying nothing or antagonizing others with aggressive communication.

Finally, before ending the session you should review the teen's Sleep Log (Worksheet 1.3), Weekly Activity and Exercise Action Plan (Worksheet I.1), Thought Record with Challenges (Worksheet 4.2), and Relaxation Skills Practice Log (Worksheet 3.3) and provide them with new worksheets for the coming week. (For additional copies of these worksheets, go to the TreatmentsThatWork™ website at www.oup.com/CHIRP.) Remember, it is important to be clinically sensitive and not overwhelm the teen with too many worksheets at one time. Continue to use your clinical judgment in prioritizing which worksheets are the most valuable for the teen at any given point in treatment with CHIRP.

Assigning Homework

As determined to be necessary based on previous response to homework assignment, have the teen and parent(s) complete the following homework assignments and bring to the next session:

- Continue filling out Worksheet 1.3: Sleep Log.
- Continue filling out Worksheet 4.2: Thought Record with Challenges.
- Continue filling out Worksheet 3.3: Relaxation Skills Practice Log.
- Complete Worksheet 7.6: Assertiveness Opportunities.
- Complete Worksheet 7.7: Talking with Others About Your Illness.
- Refine/Implement Worksheet I.1: Activity and Exercise Action Plan.

Sidebar 7.1 Talking to Others

The following is an example of talking about one's illness with others: Basir is a 17-year-old boy who has not attended school for the past 2 months due to chronic fatigue and persistent headaches. He stopped going to basketball practice and has had very little contact with peers beyond his younger brother. Basir recently began attending partial school days under a 504 Plan that was recommended by his psychologist and primary physician.

While accompanying his mother to the grocery store after school one day, Basir was approached by a former teammate from his high school basketball team. His friend asked why Basir had not been at school as much and missed team practices. Basir initially felt uncomfortable at being put on the spot, unsure of what to say. He then considered that his friend may be asking out of genuine concern, and, after thanking his friend for checking in, Basir explained, "My doctor diagnosed me with a condition that causes chronic fatigue and pain, which has made it hard for me to get through the school day, much less put in 2 hours of practice after classes. I've been out of the loop, but I am working on getting back into my routine at school and hopefully one day with basketball, too. I sure have missed it." Later in the week, Basir received a text from his friend asking him to attend the home game together that weekend. Basir was feeling more energized and confident now that he was doing a bit more, so he asked to borrow his mother's car for a few of hours to meet his friend at the game.

CHAPTER 8 Session 8: Family Roles, Communication, and Support

Family-Focused Session

Session Format

After meeting with the teen individually to go over their homework using Worksheet 7.5: Assertiveness Guidelines and Worksheet 7.6: Assertiveness Opportunities, meet together with teen and their parent(s).

Goals of the Session

- Review homework with the aim of identifying areas of difficulty, emerging themes, and progress based on completion of logs and monitoring forms assigned at the last session.
- Define parental and teen roles within the family system.
- Examine the impact of teen illness on familial roles.
- Introduce and discuss "Misguided Support."

Assertiveness and Communication About Illness

Take time to review the homework assignments individually with the teen; these assignments included Worksheet 7.5: Assertiveness Guidelines and Worksheet 7.6: Assertiveness Opportunities to track assertive communication outside of session. Collaborate with the teen to identify and troubleshoot barriers/challenges to applying assertive communication outside of session and discussing their illness with others using Worksheet 7.7: Talking with Others About Your Illness.

The use of role play exercises in session can be particularly helpful in promoting greater skill and confidence in requesting, refusing, and rebutting skills and facilitating generalization to real-life applications.

Define Parental and Teen Roles Within Family System

After meeting with the teen individually to focus on assertiveness skills, invite the parent(s) into the session to focus on family functioning. Throughout the subsequent activities, it is important that you distinguish between an *acute* versus *chronic* illness as it pertains to family roles. As emphasized previously, frequently, family members unwittingly enter into roles that are not helpful in the face of chronic illness. For example, responses to an acute episode such as restricting activity, remaining in the home, and limiting peer contact are deleterious over the course of a protracted illness. Therefore, adopting a chronic illness perspective allows families to adjust their approach accordingly. This proactive stance in facilitating coping and recovery emphasizes increased adolescent independence and social stimulation to avoid undermining the teen's self-confidence.

The list of parental roles in the "Playing a Part: The Role of Family Members" section of the Teen and Family Workbook illustrate healthy interactions that provide the teen with emotional and tangible support without undermining the development of increased teen independence in decision making, social relationships, and academic performance. Based on the age of the teen and their cognitive abilities, it is important to guide the parents in a discussion of reasonable expectations to have for their child both within and outside the context of their illness.

Parents vary considerably in their definitions of these roles, and therefore you should guide them in developing a more accurate and healthier set of expectations. By this point in treatment, you will be more aware of the family dynamics that are guiding the teen's functioning—dynamics that can range from overprotective and enmeshed to authoritarian and rejecting. In a family where parental behaviors may be undermining teen independence, treatment may place more emphasis on roles that focus on facilitating increased teen autonomy (e.g., maintaining boundaries, delegating responsibilities, providing opportunities for mastery). In an authoritarian family dynamic, emphasis may be placed on enhancing warmth and increasing parental support and reinforcement of teen independence. These roles are often fueled by parental anxiety and insecurity in the case of the overly protective/enmeshed parent or the belief that the teen should be "able to handle it on their own" in the case of a more authoritarian parental dynamic. In either case, it will be beneficial to explore parental responses to the clinician-directed role changes to be made in the service of improving teen functioning and independence.

Examine the Impact of Teen Illness on Familial Roles

Next, you will guide family members in examining the roles they have adopted in coping with the teen's chronic illness, identifying the unique challenges they each face, and generating more helpful and healthier roles that they can play. This discussion is best facilitated by getting the teen and family to identify a frustrating situation that they have faced regarding the teen's illness, which they should have done by completing Worksheet 8.1: Family Roles for homework to bring to the session. During this exchange, observe the level of independence granted to the teen and assess interparental consistency and cohesiveness. Sometimes focusing on the parents' role and behavior first will reduce the pressure on the teen, allowing them to be more comfortable with examining their own roles within the family. The goal of this activity is to encourage the teen and parent(s) to respectfully communicate with one another in the process of negotiating more helpful roles that each family member can adopt. Overall, this exercise aims to establish appropriate boundaries and clear expectations while also acknowledging the challenges to the family in the face of chronic illness.

Introduce and Discuss Misguided Support

Next, you will be introducing the concept of misguided support with the aim of helping the patient and family members understand how behaviors that were intended to be supportive may, in fact, have had an unintended impact (e.g., making the adolescent feel invalidated in their need for independence, less confident in their abilities, perhaps conflicted with both feeling more dependent on parents yet resentful). We often refer to this as a "slippery slope" in that parents often are responding appropriately to the acute illness scenario, but fail to adjust their responses as needed when the illness takes on a more chronic course. The same is true for teens. It is important that neither the teen nor the parent(s) is blamed or made to feel guilty for this phenomenon. Instead it is best depicted as a frequent and inadvertent outcome of dealing with chronic illness. Whether support has been perceived as "too much" or "too little," guide the family in recognizing the unforeseen consequences of support that has been misguided.

Refer back to the frustrating situation the family identified in Worksheet 8.1 when exploring their roles in coping with the teen's chronic illness and identify types of support that were provided (helpful, misguided, excessive, insufficient). Employing Worksheet 8.2: Did the Support "Hit the Target" for You? will guide family members in processing their response to each type of support. During this exercise, elicit intentions and reactions from each family member in order to increase mutual understanding and correct misperceptions. Ultimately, this interchange can serve as a foundation for future discussions involving more effective communication and feedback as difficulties emerge. It will be helpful to review with parents the general ways of providing support that are more likely to be perceived by teens as helpful while encouraging independence. Refer to "Getting Misguided Support Back on Target" in Chapter 8 of the Workbook.

After reviewing these general guidelines for offering helpful support, parents and teens will begin learning about more specific skills to enhance parent–teen communication. For homework, the family will review the "Talk, Talk, Talk: Improving Parent–Teen Communication" material in Session 8 of the Workbook, which illustrates the role that strong beliefs play in shaping communication and familial interaction. The examples of parental and teen beliefs included in the Workbook serve as a stimulus for the identification of their own strong beliefs as well as the statements and behaviors these beliefs generate. Parents are to complete Worksheet 8.3: My Strong Beliefs (Parent), and the teen completes Worksheet 8.4: My Strong Beliefs (Teen) to facilitate the process of each family member identifying their own distorted beliefs that they bring to their interactions and which lead to misunderstanding and misguided support. Finally, have all family members complete Worksheet 8.5: Changing Negative Communications to Positive to assist them in identifying their own and other's negative communication behaviors and the associated more effective positive alternatives. All of these activities serve to provide a wealth of clinical material for identifying and addressing sources of stress and tension in family interactions that may undermine conflict resolution, problem solving, and other barriers to teen independent functioning.

Finally, before ending the session you should review the teen's Sleep Log (Worksheet 1.3), Weekly Activity and Exercise Action Plan (Worksheet I.1), Thought Record with Challenges (Worksheet 4.2), and Relaxation Skills Practice Log (Worksheet 3.3) and provide them with new worksheets for the coming week. (For additional copies of these worksheets, go to the TreatmentsThatWork™ website at www.oup.com/CHIRP.) Remember, it is important to be clinically sensitive and not overwhelm the teen with too many worksheets at one time. Continue to use your clinical judgment in prioritizing which worksheets are the most valuable for the teen at any given point in treatment with the Children's Health and Illness Recovery Program (CHIRP).

CHIRP: Going Forward

Session 8 is the last session in CHIRP to introduce new material to the teen and family. Session 9 provides an overview of the skills and practices introduced via CHIRP to date while reinforcing key practices to prevent regression and relapse in functioning. The remaining sessions will be used for assisting the teen and their parents in applying, revisiting, and refining the skills learned in CHIRP in their daily life with the goal of making these tools a natural response in improving teen functioning and quality of life when dealing with fluctuations in their health. As reported in our outcomes research, many of the teens and their families who continue to apply CHIRP skills in their daily lives report improvement in the teen's functioning physically, academically, and socially (including improvement in symptoms of pain and fatigue), and they continue to improve beyond completion of CHIRP for months to years later.

Assigning Homework

As determined to be necessary based on previous response to homework assignment, have the teen and parent(s) complete the following homework assignments and bring to the next session:

- Continue filling out Worksheet 1.3: Sleep Log.
- Continue filling out Worksheet 4.2: Thought Record with Challenges.
- Continue filling out Worksheet 3.3: Relaxation Skills Practice Log.
- Refine/Implement Worksheet I.1: Activity and Exercise Action Plan.
- Improving Parent–Teen Communication. As directed by your CHIRP clinician, it can be helpful to continue using the Worksheets (8.3, 8.4, and 8.5) from this session to work on your Strong Beliefs, Misguided Support, and Negative versus Positive Communications.

Sidebar 8.1

Angelina is a 16-year-old girl whose asthma has resulted in her being unable to attend school for several weeks. Her parents are concerned about Angelina falling behind in her schoolwork and missing out on play practice with the local theater group. In the session with their CHIRP clinician, Angelina seems rather passive and quiet, yet becomes visibly annoyed when her father expresses concern that she may lose out on an opportunity to apply for a drama scholarship that he has learned about. When her father asks Angelina about her plans, she tearfully states, "You just don't get it! I'm not going to get *any* scholarships, and probably won't get into college anyway."

Her father, visibly upset himself, states, "With that attitude, you're probably right. You just don't seem to appreciate any of the things we do for you to help you plan for your future." At this point, Angelina buries her face between her folded arms and sobs. Angelina's mother scoots her chair over next to the teen and puts her arm around her daughter, but Angelina doesn't respond. At this point, the CHIRP clinician reminds the family of the material they have covered about misguided support. She asks each family member to describe the kind of support Angelina needs in this situation and how the support provided in the session missed the target. The CHIRP clinician encourages Angelina to identify the feelings and thoughts she was having when her father talked about the drama scholarship, with particular emphasis on the strong beliefs that Angela holds, which might be fueling her emotional reaction ("My dad just doesn't understand or seem to care. He just wants me to get a scholarship and save some money"). The father is asked to identify his strong beliefs (catastrophic fear that Angelina may not go to college: "I have to solve this problem or Angelina may ruin her chances for a successful future"), which may be driving his behavior.

The clinician then helps Angelina and her parents in reconstructing their interactions and generating more realistic beliefs. In the case of Angelina's father, the clinician focuses on identifying his thought as catastrophic in nature and exploring alternative (and more realistic) outcomes, such as the belief that with time and support (as opposed to added pressure), Angelina is more likely to catch up on her school work and go on to experience a fun and meaningful end to high school and start of college. With Angelina, the clinician focuses on creating a more flexible interpretation of her father's behavior by understanding the role that his strong beliefs play in his reaction and recognizing his genuine concern about her future, as opposed to merely saving money. With a better understanding of the others' intentions, both Angelina and her father are able to communicate in a more productive manner about helpful ways to engage in supportive interactions.

CHAPTER 9 Session 9: Keys to Maintaining Progress

Session Format

Review homework with family and meet with teen individually to review skills application.

Goals of the Session

- Review homework with the aim of identifying areas of difficulty, emerging themes, and progress based on completion of logs and monitoring forms assigned at the last session.
- Discuss "Keys to Recovery and Long-Term Wellness."
- Review "Working Towards a Normal Daily Schedule."

Improving Parent–Teen Communication

For homework, the family was responsible for reviewing the Workbook Session 8 material "Talk, Talk, Talk: Improving Parent–Teen Communication," which illustrates the role that strong beliefs play in shaping communication and familial interaction. Parents were to complete Worksheet 8.3: My Strong Beliefs (Parent), and teens were to complete Worksheet 8.4: My Strong Beliefs (Teen) to facilitate their becoming more aware of the strong and often distorted beliefs that drive unproductive feelings and behaviors that often lead to misguided support and undermine more appropriate teen independence. Take time to review examples of strong beliefs and discuss those identified by both parent and teen from their homework. Employing the teen's and parent's responses to homework in completing Worksheet 8.5: Changing Negative Communications to Positive, discuss the negative and positive communication styles identified by the teen and parent. Ensure that both parent and teen are considering their own patterns of communicating in addition to those of other family members. Worksheet 8.5 can be very useful as a reference during family discussions to help the teen and parent identify times when they are using a negative pattern of communication while having a ready reference to the more positive alternative response. Focus should be given to on-the-spot rephrasing of negative statements into a positive alternative format. Encourage the family to keep the Worksheet 8.5 communication patterns in an accessible place at home, where they can refer (even humorously at times) to these strategies during the week and employ them in altering their maladaptive communication practices.

Discuss Keys to Recovery and Long-Term Wellness

The main focus of this session is to establish key principles and practices for long-term improved functioning. Several important areas to discuss include

- a plan for physical exercise and activity,
- establishing family rules for communicating about symptoms,
- reasonable expectations for daily activity (including school attendance), and
- a plan for continuing to follow-up with specialists and clinicians as part of the teen's multidisciplinary treatment team.

The cornerstone of this session is the teen and family's understanding of the rationale for working toward a normal daily schedule. This has been a recurrent theme throughout the course of the Children's Health and Illness Recovery Program (CHIRP), and it should be clear at this point that the goal in doing so is to minimize the deleterious effects of prolonged restriction from academic, social, and physical activity whenever symptoms are present. It has been shown that full resolution of symptoms is not sufficient or necessary for chronically ill teens to improve their functioning. In fact, it is increasing functioning that most often leads to reductions in symptom severity. This is thought to occur via mechanisms of increased physical conditioning, distraction provided by engagement in activities and involvements, and possible reversal of central sensitization reactivity.

When discussing goals of the long-term recovery plan, it is important to put them in writing. Goals should be clear and measurable. At times it may be useful to establish rewards for meeting goals; a written contract may even be useful in such instances. The long-term improved functioning plan should be tailored to address the issues that have emerged over the course of the CHIRP intervention.

Discuss Working Toward a Normal Daily Schedule

After reviewing the keys to long-term improved functioning and defining goals, help the teen and family establish a daily schedule that matches developmentally typical teen experiences as closely as possible. While emphasis has been placed on function, as opposed to symptoms, throughout the course of CHIRP, it is important that the family continue to adjust their expectations for functioning as they acquire new skills, gain confidence, and reduce disability. Discuss the various components of a normal daily schedule and clearly define expectations for functioning in areas of sleep hygiene, personal hygiene, meals, school, and at-home activities.

Finally, before ending the session you should review the teen's Sleep Log (Worksheet 1.3), Weekly Activity and Exercise Action Plan (Worksheet I.1), Thought Record with Challenges (Worksheet 4.2), and Relaxation Skills Practice Log (Worksheet 3.3) and provide them with new worksheets for the coming week. (For additional copies of these worksheets, go to the TreatmentsThatWork™ website at www.oup.com/CHIRP.) Remember, it is important to be clinically sensitive and not overwhelm the teen with too many worksheets at one time. Continue to use your clinical judgment in prioritizing which worksheets are the most valuable for the teen at any given point in treatment with CHIRP.

Assigning Homework

As determined to be necessary based on previous response to homework assignment, have the teen and parent(s) complete the following homework assignments and bring to the next session:

- Continue filling out Worksheet 1.3: Sleep Log.
- Continue filling out Worksheet 4.2: Thought Record with Challenges.

- Continue filling out Worksheet 3.3: Relaxation Skills Practice Log.
- Implement a Daily Schedule.
- Refine/Implement Worksheet I.1: Activity and Exercise Action Plan.

Sidebar 9.1

Tabitha is an 18-year-old young woman who was seen previously for sessions using CHIRP to aid in her recovery from juvenile fibromyalgia syndrome (JFM), chronic fatigue syndrome (CFS), migraine headaches, and hypoglycemia. While in the course of treatment she was eventually able to return to high school and graduate, she decided to stay at home and work rather than move away to attend college, as most of her friends had done. Her job at a clothing store in a local mall was initially enjoyable because she had an interest in fashion design. However, her competence at her job led her supervisor to increasingly rely on Tabitha to come in and cover for other employees who called in ill or had quit their job. These extra hours, including weekends, led Tabitha to feel increasingly pressured and highly fatigued when she came home after work. With most of her friends from high school away at college, she became increasingly socially isolated and lonely. Her regular exercise routine (often done with her mother at a local gym) was also disrupted by her work schedule. It didn't take long for the downward spiral of this situation to exacerbate many of her symptoms, this time accompanied by a depressed mood and significant doubt and confusion over "what I really want to do with my life."

Tabitha shared her story with the CHIRP clinician accompanied by frequent tears, expressions of discouragement, and feeling she has "let [herself] and everyone down." Tabitha and her clinician reviewed her personal schedule and rather quickly established that her balance of work, rest/relaxation, social time, sleep, exercise, etc., had become severely skewed. They also reviewed how she was having difficulty asserting herself with her supervisor, who had increasingly seemed to take for granted Tabitha's willingness to come in on short notice whenever he called her. In fact, Tabitha had never told him about her medical condition "since [she] had been doing so well."

In the course of a few sessions, Tabitha and her clinician were able to identify the strong beliefs that led the teen to conceal her prior illness from her supervisor and refrain from being assertive about her need for a less demanding and more predictable work schedule and then attacked these using the thought-challenging and thought-changing skills she had acquired in her earlier sessions. In session, the clinician and teen were able to rehearse and role play Tabitha's approach to her supervisor who, when Tabitha actually spoke with him, was quite understanding and accommodating in order to keep his "most valued employee." Tabitha was also able to identify her need to develop new peer social relationships to replace those lost when her friends left for college. Her symptoms decreased significantly when she was once again able to orchestrate a more balanced lifestyle.

CHAPTER 10 Sessions 10–12: Skill Reinforcement and Relapse Prevention

Sessions 10–12 of the Children's Health and Illness Recovery Program (CHIRP) are less structured to allow you to tailor interventions to the teen/family's or group's current needs. Focus should be on reviewing, consolidating, and actively applying the skills learned in CHIRP that are most pertinent to ongoing treatment needs and level of functioning (accounting for progress and remaining challenges).

Includes Family-Focused Session 3: As the CHIRP clinician, use your clinical judgment to determine the balance between conducting individual teen, parent, and conjoint parent–teen sessions for the remainder of the CHIRP intervention. Every teen and family will have unique needs and dynamics, and the flexibility built into the remaining sessions is intended to allow the clinician to tailor additional interventions accordingly. It is advised that at least one of the sessions be a conjoint family session in order to address the many family-based interventions introduced in CHIRP that are critical to establishing a path to increased teen independent functioning.

Session Format

Of the three remaining CHIRP sessions, at least one (or more, if needed) should be with the teen and parents conjointly for a third formal conjoint family session. Of course, clinical judgment will inform the need for more or less parental involvement. It will be beneficial to include parents for at least a portion of the teen sessions in order to review relevant teen strategies and homework.

Goals of the Session

- Review homework with the aim of identifying areas of difficulty, emerging themes, and progress based on completion of logs and monitoring forms from previous sessions.
- Revisit components of CHIRP that the teen and parent(s) have had difficulty applying and mastering.
- Construct and revise/refine Worksheet 10.1: My Long-Term Recovery and Wellness Plan.
- Anticipate and discuss relapse prevention and response strategies.

The main focus of this and subsequent sessions is to proactively problem-solve ways for the teen and family to handle potential future exacerbations of their symptoms. As homework for this session, the teen and parent(s) should complete Worksheet 10.1: My Long-Term Recovery and Wellness Plan, which you will review with the teen and family conjointly in their session. Life is stressful, and stress can never be fully avoided. This has been a recurrent theme throughout CHIRP and should be strongly emphasized during the final stages of formal treatment; indeed, the ultimate goal of CHIRP is to empower the teen and their family to gain a sense of mastery and internalized locus of control in managing the challenges that will inevitably emerge.

While the formal CHIRP sessions may be coming to an end, the importance of continuing to utilize the knowledge and skills learned in the program cannot be overstated because this will be an essential component to sustained improvement in the context of long-term functioning. Exacerbation of symptoms and decreases in functioning may occur. Families can be encouraged to contact you for booster sessions should this occur; however, care should be taken not to reinforce excessive dependence and/or overreliance on external solutions. From this standpoint, it can often be helpful to predict the recurrence of symptoms as well as potential changes in functioning while prompting the teen and family to proactively generate a plan for (1) decreasing the likelihood of major setbacks and (2) applying relevant coping skills to effectively manage the anticipated challenges. Communication between the teen and their parent(s) regarding worsening of symptoms or functioning will be key in avoiding longer term regression and relapse.

While at this point the bulk of the activities in the manualized CHIRP treatment may have been accomplished, there is great variability in teen and family readiness for discharge. While recovery from chronic pediatric health conditions is highly variable and for some may be a lifelong challenge, many patients and their families may desire or need additional sessions to reinforce their application of the skills and practices introduced over the course of this treatment program. Clinical judgment will be required in determining whether an extension of treatment is warranted. Factors to consider when deciding whether to continue include possible dependency, level of teen confidence in applying skills, tolerance for and acceptance of persistent symptoms, and level of parental need for support and guidance in instilling confident independence in their teen. Complicating factors to be aware of include the emergence of major stressors/crises, inadequate support to maintain gains, and/or other teen/parent psychological factors that may be impacting readiness for discharge. In either case, a clear rationale for extended treatment should be present, and remaining therapy goals will need to be clarified and defined in concrete terms if treatment is to be extended.

Appendix A

Model 504 Letter

This is an example of a letter to a patient's school to initiate the process of establishing a working advocacy relationship via a 504 Plan.

I am writing at the request of the parents of JLC, currently a senior at your school. As a specialist in pediatric psychology, I have been following JLC for several months, along with her pediatric specialists and physical therapist, to facilitate her rehabilitation and recovery from a debilitating medical condition.

As you know, JLC has had a rather arduous recovery process from transverse myelitis, a neurological disorder caused by inflammation across both sides of one level, or segment, of the spinal cord. The term *myelitis* refers to inflammation of the spinal cord; *transverse* simply describes the position of the inflammation, that is, across the width of the spinal cord. Attacks of inflammation can damage or destroy myelin, the fatty insulating substance that covers nerve cell fibers. This damage causes nervous system scars that interrupt communications between the nerves in the spinal cord and the rest of the body. Fortunately, JLC's doctors have evaluated her medical condition to have a favorable prognosis. However, a national specialist in transverse myelitis at _____ Hospital has predicted that it may take up to a year or two for full recovery, and perhaps longer.

Most recently, while her pain symptoms have improved, JLC has developed neurocognitive difficulties that adversely affect her ability to concentrate, accompanied by decreased short-term memory, impaired organization, and impaired ability to sustain activity on tasks. These cognitive symptoms, which may be related to both her disease and/or changes in medications, create problems that likely affect her mental efficiency and ability to perform up to previous levels of achievement in school. These concentration difficulties, at least in the short term, may affect her ability to learn and have an adverse impact on her academic performance beyond the impact of such factors as absence due to illness.

We have found that making accommodations (preferably under a formal 504 Plan) to give the student allowance for these deficits is crucial to both the illness recovery process as well as to bolstering the teen's self-esteem and self-confidence. In my experience to date, I have found JLC to be a highly conscientious teen who has some difficulty asking for help, tending to expect the most from herself despite the limitations imposed by her medical condition. We have found the following accommodations beneficial for patients with these neurocognitive complications to their illness:

- Allowing the student to either start her school day a bit later or have a study hall as her first class so she can ease into the demands of the school day;
- Allowing extended time or untimed conditions on selected assignments and tests;
- Taking an online class in order to minimize in-school time and demands on her decreased concentration skills;
- Reducing overall workload;
- Seating away from distractions;
- Having access to another student's class notes;
- Providing the student with alternative activities for gym class such as less strenuous walking or a self-directed exercise routine;
- Providing the student with a point-person with whom they can check in on a regular basis and who is routinely updated about the student's health condition and can thus advocate for their educational accommodation needs; and
- Supplementing written assignments and essay exams with oral exams and reports.

Additionally, the painfulness of JLC's condition makes sitting for periods longer than 15–20 minutes difficult, if not impossible. Her level of pain often makes it difficult for her to concentrate on the academic task at hand. It would be most beneficial if she could be allowed to stand and even walk back and forth periodically to prevent these painful episodes, perhaps near the back of the classroom where it would be less distracting to the other students. A desk or platform adjusted to her standing height would allow her to actually do some of her work while standing.

While I have encouraged JLC to be more assertive and proactive in approaching her teachers when she needs assistance or accommodation, I fear that her tendency toward perfectionism has made her reluctant to ask for what she would consider special considerations. Hopefully, with these accommodations in place, she will be less reluctant to access them.

I am happy to be available to you, via phone, email, or a scheduled meeting at the school, to better tailor these factors to meet JLC's needs over the course of her senior year.

Thank you.

Appendix B

CHIRP Mastery Rating Scales

MASTERY RATING SCALE—TEEN REPORT

Participant ID: ______________________ Date completed: __________________

Please rate how much you believe you have mastered the skills below since starting CHIRP. Using the following scale, please choose ONE number that best fits how well you learned the skill.

0—I do not understand this skill.

1—I understand this skill.

2—I practiced this skill in the CHIRP session (or group).

3—I used this skill outside of the CHIRP session (or group) at least once.

4—I used this skill on more than one occasion in an actual life situation.

STRESS MANAGEMENT

____________ 1. I identified stressors in my life.

____________ 2. I recognized stress in my body.

PROBLEM SOLVING

____________ 3. I identified a problem that needed to be solved.

____________ 4. I developed a plan for solving the problem.

____________ 5. I put my plan into action and evaluated the outcome.

TIME MANAGEMENT AND PRIORITIZING

_____________ 6. I have been able to tell the difference between my "want to's" and "have to's."

_____________ 7. I created a realistic schedule for myself and followed it.

INTERPERSONAL RELATIONSHIPS

_____________ 8. I have identified the important people in my life.

_____________ 9. I have had a conversation with someone I didn't know.

_____________ 10. I recognized my strengths and weaknesses when communicating with others.

ASSERTIVENESS

_____________ 11. I requested help from someone else when I needed it.

_____________ 12. I said "no" to someone to keep from taking on too much.

_____________ 13. When I disagreed with another person, I spoke up and shared my feelings.

_____________ 14. I talked with someone else about my illness.

RELAXATION SKILLS

_____________ 15. I used diaphragmatic breathing.

_____________ 16. I used progressive muscle relaxation.

_____________ 17. I used imagery.

THOUGHT-CHALLENGING SKILLS

_____________ 18. I recognized the relationship between my thoughts, feelings, and behaviors.

_____________ 19. I recognized negative automatic thoughts that weren't helpful.

_____________ 20. I replaced my negative thoughts with more realistic and helpful thoughts.

COMMUNICATION

_______________ 21. I communicated openly with a family member about what I need and don't need.

_______________ 22. I identified my "strong beliefs" that got in the way of effective communication.

_______________ 23. I found myself communicating in a negative way, caught it, and used positive communication instead.

_______________ 24. I actively listened to a person in a conversation without interrupting.

MASTERY RATING SCALE—PARENT REPORT

Participant ID: ________________ Date completed: ________________

Please rate how much you believe your teen has mastered the skills below since starting CHIRP.

Using the following scale, please choose ONE number that best fits how well your teen learned the skill.

0—My teen does not understand this skill.

1—My teen understands this skill.

2—My teen practiced this skill in their CHIRP session (or group).

3—My teen used this skill outside of their CHIRP session (or group) at least once.

4—My teen used this skill on more than one occasion in a real-life situation.

STRESS MANAGEMENT

__________ 1. My teen identified stressors in their life.

__________ 2. My teen recognized stress in their body.

PROBLEM SOLVING

__________ 3. My teen identified a problem that needed to be solved.

__________ 4. My teen developed a plan for solving the problem.

__________ 5. My teen put their plan into action and evaluated the outcome.

TIME MANAGEMENT AND PRIORITIZING

__________ 6. My teen has been able to tell the difference between their "want to's" and "have to's."

__________ 7. My teen created a realistic schedule for themselves and followed it.

INTERPERSONAL RELATIONSHIPS

__________ 8. My teen has identified the important people in their life.

__________ 9. My teen has had a conversation with someone they didn't know.

__________ 10. My teen recognized their strengths and weaknesses when communicating with others.

ASSERTIVENESS

_____________ 11. My teen requested help from someone else when they needed it.

_____________ 12. My teen said "no" to someone to keep from taking on too much.

_____________ 13. When my teen disagreed with another person, they spoke up and shared their feelings.

_____________ 14. My teen talked with someone else about their illness.

RELAXATION SKILLS

_____________ 15. My teen used diaphragmatic breathing.

_____________ 16. My teen used progressive muscle relaxation.

_____________ 17. My teen used imagery.

THOUGHT-CHALLENGING SKILLS

_____________ 18. My teen recognized the relationship between their thoughts, feelings, and behaviors.

_____________ 19. My teen recognized negative automatic thoughts that weren't helpful.

_____________ 20. My teen replaced their negative thoughts with more realistic and helpful thoughts.

COMMUNICATION

_____________ 21. My teen communicated openly with a family member about what they need and don't need.

_____________ 22. My teen identified their "strong beliefs" that got in the way of effective communication.

_____________ 23. My teen found that they were communicating in a negative way, caught it, and used positive communication instead.

_____________ 24. My teen actively listened to a person in a conversation without interrupting.

MASTERY RATING SCALE—CLINICIAN REPORT

Participant ID: ____________________ Date completed: ____________________

Please rate how much you believe the teen has mastered the skills below since starting CHIRP. Using the following scale, please choose ONE number that best fits how well the teen learned the skill.

0—The teen does not understand this skill.

1—The teen understands this skill.

2—The teen practiced this skill in their CHIRP session (or group).

3—The teen used this skill outside of their CHIRP session (or group) at least once.

4—The teen used this skill on more than one occasion in a real-life situation.

STRESS MANAGEMENT

____________ 1. The teen identified stressors in their life.

____________ 2. The teen recognized stress in their body.

PROBLEM SOLVING

____________ 3. The teen identified a problem that needed to be solved.

____________ 4. The teen developed a plan for solving the problem.

____________ 5. The teen put their plan into action and evaluated the outcome.

TIME MANAGEMENT AND PRIORITIZING

____________ 6. The teen has been able to tell the difference between their "want to's" and "have to's."

____________ 7. The teen created a realistic schedule for themselves and followed it.

INTERPERSONAL RELATIONSHIPS

____________ 8. The teen has identified the important people in their life.

____________ 9. The teen has had a conversation with someone they didn't know.

____________ 10. The teen recognized their strengths and weaknesses when communicating with others.

ASSERTIVENESS

_____________ 11. The teen requested help from someone else when they needed it.

_____________ 12. The teen said "no" to someone to keep from taking on too much.

_____________ 13. When the teen disagreed with another person, they spoke up and shared their feelings.

_____________ 14. The teen talked with someone else about their illness.

RELAXATION SKILLS

_____________ 15. The teen used diaphragmatic breathing.

_____________ 16. The teen used progressive muscle relaxation.

_____________ 17. The teen used imagery.

THOUGHT-CHALLENGING SKILLS

_____________ 18. The teen recognized the relationship between their thoughts, feelings, and behaviors.

_____________ 19. The teen recognized negative automatic thoughts that weren't helpful.

_____________ 20. The teen replaced their negative thoughts with more realistic and helpful thoughts.

COMMUNICATION

_____________ 21. The teen communicated openly with a family member about what they need and don't need.

_____________ 22. The teen identified their "strong beliefs" that got in the way of effective communication.

_____________ 23. The teen found that they were communicating in a negative way, caught it, and used positive communication instead.

_____________ 24. The teen actively listened to a person in a conversation without interrupting.

Appendix C

CHIRP Program Brochure

What Patients & Parents Say About CHIRP

"Through this program I learned to be more patient, to cope with the stresses of my illness and to balance my life's activities. This allowed me to gradually become more active, get back to school and begin to enjoy my life again."

- *Denise, age 16*

"We worked together as a family to better understand Denise's illness, to give her more independence in managing her recovery and day-to-day life, and to advocate with her school to make sure her educational needs were met. Most of all, we developed a sense of hope and persistence in helping her get her life back."

- *Denise's Mother*

Evidence-Based Treatment

CHIRP employs a structured treatment approach that helps teens develop specific skills in identifying and managing the stresses that come with chronic illness. Outcomes research has led to the CHIRP CLINICIAN HANDBOOK and the CHIRP PATIENT & FAMILY WORKBOOK being published by Oxford University Press in their *Treatments That Work* series. Our patients and families who have completed the 12-session CHIRP intervention report improvement in independent functioning and overall quality of life.

CHIRP

(YOUR ADDRESS AND REFERRAL INFORMATION HERE)

CHIRP

Children's
Health &
Illness
Recovery
Program

An Effective Program to Facilitate Recovery of Functioning in Teens with Chronic Illness

What is CHIRP & who will benefit?

CHIRP is a structured multidisciplinary program, based on research and clinical experience with pediatric patients with chronic painful and fatiguing illnesses. The program is specifically designed for adolescents (12 to 18) experiencing difficulty maintaining a more active lifestyle while coping with and recovering from their illness.

While many teens who benefit from this program have been diagnosed with Chronic Fatigue Syndrome, Fibromyalgia, Dysautonomia or Postural Orthostatic Tachycardia Syndrome (POTS), those with functional decline associated with other chronic illnesses may benefit.

Difficulties experienced by teens dealing with these conditions typically include the following:

- Excessive fatigue
- Low energy, stamina & endurance
- Widespread pain in more than one area of the body
- Frequent headaches
- Light-headedness, dizziness, fainting
- Non-refreshing/dys-regulated sleep
- Frequent school absences
- Difficulty with concentration, short-term memory, planning or organizing
- Decline or difficulty with academic and/or social functioning
- Decreased self-confidence/motivation

How it works

CHIRP establishes a collaborative relationship between the physician, pediatric specialist, physical/occupational therapist, pediatric health psychologist, school and the patient's family to create a program targeting key symptoms and functional limitations. Interventions are designed to facilitate the development of coping and recovery strategies for both the patient and family.

CHIRP has two primary goals. The first goal is to educate and support the patient, family, and others in the community in the understanding of these painful and fatiguing pediatric conditions. The second goal is to establish effective interventions that facilitate skill development in the following areas:

*Understanding and communicating about illness and symptoms
* Identifying and managing illness- and non-illness related stress
*Coping and problem-solving
*Time management and prioritizing
*Improving sleep hygiene
*Improving self-expression, communication and assertiveness
*Relaxation and self-soothing
*Developing helpful family roles for enhancing independence and communication
*Advocating for appropriate educational needs and accommodations
*Developing effective long-term recovery practices and lifestyle modifications

Making a Referral

Any pediatrician, family practitioner or pediatric specialist may refer a patient to CHIRP by calling the phone number below or completing a referral form and mailing/faxing it, with appropriate releases. Upon receipt of the referral we will contact you to gather more relevant clinical information before scheduling an evaluation.

Phone:
Fax:

CHIRP
(YOUR ADDRESS AND CONTACT INFORMATION HERE)

Appendix D

CHIRP Physician Referral Form

CHIRP Physician Referral Form
Please attach a recent clinical summary.

Referral Source

Referring physician:	Date:
Address:	Phone:
	Fax:
	Email:

Patient Information

Patient name:	Gender:	DOB:
Address:	Phone:	
Parent name:	Insurance info:	

Diagnoses:

____

____

____

____

Reason for referral and pertinent information:

____

____

____

____

____

____

____

____

Fax to: ____

at ( )____
(include signed release form)
Children's Health and Illness Recovery Program (CHIRP)

Address: ____

____

____

____

Appendix E

CHIRP Interdisciplinary Communication Form

CHIRP Interdisciplinary Communication Form

Patient name: ___________________________ Date: ___________________________

DOB: __________________ CHIRP start date: _________________

Diagnoses:

____

____

____

CHIRP Status in Treatment Program

Circled items have been completed by the teen in the CHIRP intervention.

Areas completed:

Stress Identification and Management
- Identifying Stress and Stressors
- List of Teen Stressors
- Recognizing Stress in Your Body
- Monitoring Stress
- Controlling Stress with Coping

Problem-Focused Coping
- Problem-Solving Skills
- Time Management and Prioritizing
- Interpersonal & Assertiveness Skills
- Talking with Others About Your Illness

Emotion-Focused Coping
- Thought-Challenging Skills
- Relaxation Skills & Imagery
- Coping Menu

Independent Functioning
- Playing a Part: Family Roles
- Misguided Support
- Parent-Teen Communication
- Contracting for Behavior Change
- Improving Independent Functioning
- Impact on Independent Functioning

Long-Term Coping & Recovery

Narrative feedback of current patient status:

____

____

____

____

____

____

Current treatment plan:

____

____

____

____

____

____

Primary MD:

Provider name: ____

Phone/Fax: ____

Specialists:

Provider name: ____

Phone/Fax: ____

CHIRP Clinician:

Name: ______________________________

Phone: ________________________

Fax:____________________

Email:_____________________________________

Appendix F

CHIRP Feedback Form

CHIRP Feedback Form

Please complete and fax this form to:

Children's Health and Illness Recovery Program

Address: ______________________________

Phone: ______________________________

Fax: ______________________________

Email: ______________________________

Patient name: ____________________ Date: ____________________

DOB: ____________________

Diagnoses:

____

____

____

____

____

____

Please use the space below to provide us with any important information regarding your evaluation and treatment of this patient. Your input is extremely valuable to our understanding of this patient's current status and needs, as well as to help us monitor rehabilitation progress.

Narrative feedback of current patient status:

____

____

____

____

____

____

Current treatment plans:

____

____

____

____

____

____

____________________ ____________________

Printed name Signature

Phone: ________________ Date: ______________

Appendix G

Suggested Assessment Measures

Coping Behaviors and Skills

Child Observation Coping Scale (COCS; 57 items; Kronenberger et al., 1996; Kronenberger, 2003). The COCS is a 57-item parent-report questionnaire of coping in 19 domains: Denial, Information Seeking, Self-Blame, Social Withdrawal, Regression, Somatization, Religion, Distraction, Complaining, Cognitive Restructuring, Social Support, Humor, Avoidance, Activity Compensation, Emotional Upset, Resignation, Wishful Thinking, Problem Solving, and Externalizing/Displacement. Caregivers rate the frequency of child coping behaviors on a 0 (Not at all), 1 (Sometimes), 2 (Often) scale, based on either the child's typical coping behaviors (general version of COCS), coping behaviors related to stress of illness (illness version of COCS), or coping behaviors related to a specific stressor named by the caregiver or clinician (specific version of COCS). COCS subscale scores are the mean of the three item ratings for each subscale. Norms are not available for the COCS, but studies with samples of children with cancer (as well as with healthy children) suggest that mean COCS subscale scores range from a low of 0.30 (for Self-Blame) to a high of 1.18 (for Distraction), and most standard deviations are in approximately the 0.50 range (Kronenberger, 1993). Although interpretation of scores varies somewhat by subscale (because of different mean scores in the population), COCS subscale scores of 1.5 or higher are considered elevated (in the direction of the name of the scale) both normatively and based on item anchors (e.g., 1.5 would indicate that the average score for an item on a subscale falls between "sometimes" and "often"), whereas COCS subscale scores of 0.6 to 1.1 are considered typical or moderate; scores below 0.6 are considered to be low. A child self-report version of the COCS has been piloted but has not been well-studied (Carter, personal communication).

KIDCOPE (15 items). The KIDCOPE is an 11-item (teen version) or 15-item (child version) self-report questionnaire of 10 domains of coping: Distraction, Social Withdrawal, Cognitive Restructuring, Self-Criticism, Blaming Others, Problem Solving, Emotional Regulation,

Wishful Thinking, Social Support, and Resignation. For each item, the child states how much they did the coping behavior (frequency; on a 0–3 scale for teens and a Yes–No scale for children) and how much the coping behavior helped (efficacy; on a 0–4 scale for teens and a 0–2 scale for children). KIDCOPE items are answered in relation to a specific stressor chosen by the child or clinician. The respondent also rates how much the stressor made them nervous, sad, and angry/mad (Spirito et al., 1988). Several different methods of KIDCOPE scoring have been proposed. Each item can be treated as a separate score for frequency and efficacy of the coping behavior (e.g., Spirito et al., 1988) (for coping behaviors with two items on the child version, the higher score is typically used), or items can be combined to yield total frequency and efficacy behaviors for groups of coping behaviors (or, in some cases, frequency and efficacy scores are added together; Rodgers et al., 2012; Wagner, Ferguson, & Smith, 2012). Proposed item groupings into subscales have included positive (Cognitive Restructuring, Problem Solving, Positive Emotional Regulation [e.g., the emotional regulation item involving calming down], and Social Support) versus negative (Distraction, Social Withdrawal, Self-Criticism, Blaming Others, Negative Emotional Regulation [e.g., the emotional regulation item involving becoming upset], Wishful Thinking, and Resignation) coping (Wagner et al., 2012) and active (Distraction, Emotional Regulation, Problem Solving, Cognitive Restructuring, Social Support) versus passive (Wishful Thinking, Social Withdrawal, Resignation, Self-Criticism, and Blaming Others) coping (Rodgers et al., 2012). The KIDCOPE is one of the most widely used self-report coping scales for children.

Family Response to Child Symptoms

Health Experience and Behaviors Inventory (HEBI; Carter et al., 2002; 43 items). The HEBI is a 43-item questionnaire completed by parents/guardians regarding their attitudes toward their child's health, symptoms, and treatments. Items are answered on a 0 (Not True), 1 (Somewhat or Sometimes True), or 2 (Very True or Often True) scale. HEBI items fall into five factor analytically derived subscales: restriction/dependence (4 items, possible score range of 0–8; parent believes that it is best to restrict the child's activities and school attendance as a result of physical condition), consideration of alternative treatments (6 items, possible score range of 0–12; parent believes that conventional medical treatments are not helping and that alternative or nontraditional treatments should be considered), emotional/functional decline (7 items, possible score range of 0–14; negative social, family, functional, activity, and emotional outcomes related to having the condition), medical satisfaction (6 items, possible score range of 0–12; confidence and satisfaction in medical care), and stress sensitivity (5 items, one of which is reverse-scored, possible score range of 0–10; problems with coping and behavior related to the illness). In a large sample of children seen by a pediatric consultation-liaison service (Carter, Kronenberger, & King, 2006), HEBI scores (mean; SD) for each of the subscales were as follows: restriction/dependence (2.76; 2.21), consideration of alternative treatments (4.55; 2.37), emotional/functional decline (5.75; 3.05), medical satisfaction (7.95; 2.99), and stress sensitivity (2.85; 1.79).

Juvenile Health Experience and Behaviors Inventory (JHEBI; Carter et al., 2004; 43 items). The JHEBI is a 43-item self-report questionnaire with similar item content to the HEBI (with rewordings into first-person and simpler concepts and vocabulary). Items are answered on a 0 (Not True), 1 (Somewhat or Sometimes True), 2 (Very True or Often True) scale. JHEBI items fall into the same five subscales with the same items and scoring as the HEBI. In a large sample of children seen by a pediatric consultation-liaison service (Carter et al., 2006), JHEBI scores (mean; SD) for each of the subscales were as follows: restriction/dependence (2.91; 2.00), consideration of alternative treatments (4.58; 2.13), emotional/functional decline (5.03; 3.08), medical satisfaction (8.13; 2.72), and stress sensitivity (2.60; 1.69).

Illness-Related Functional Disability

Functional Disability Inventory (FDI; Claar & Walker, 2006; Walker & Greene, 1991; 15 items). The FDI is a 15-item rating scale of the extent to which the child has had physical difficulty performing typical daily activities over the prior 2-week period. Examples of activities evaluated by the FDI-PR include walking to the bathroom, going up stairs, riding in the school bus, being at school, playing sports, watching TV, walking, and doing homework. Each activity is rated on a 0 (no trouble) to 4 (impossible) scale. The FDI score is the sum of all items (range of 0 to 60). Parent-report (FDI-PR) and child-report (FDI-CR) versions of the FDI exist.

Life Functioning

Barkley Functional Impairment Scale—Children and Adolescents (BFIS-CA; Barkley, 2012; 23 items). The BFIS-CA is a parent-rated scale of independent adaptive, personal, and social functioning in children and adolescents during the past 6 months. Parents rate 15 areas of functioning (including family interactions, school, peers, community, money, hygiene, homework, chores/tasks, and sports) on a 0 (not at all) to 9 (severe) scale. Information about grades, sports, friends, extracurriculars, and behavior is also provided. The BFIS-CA provides scores in two broad areas: Home-School and Community. Each BFIS item, as well as the aggregate scores can be compared to norms to give a percentile score by age and gender (Barkley, 2012).

Symptom Ratings: Fatigue

Fatigue Severity Scale (FSS; Krupp, LaRocca, Muir-Nash, & Steinberg, 1989; 9 items). The FSS is a 9-item rating scale assessing severity of fatigue symptoms on a 1 (disagree) to 7 (agree) scale, as observed by the parent or self-reported by the child. Items are answered based on the past 4 weeks and assess general fatigue (e.g., being easily fatigued), fatigue in certain settings (exercise), and effects of fatigue (e.g., interfering with physical, social, or daily functioning). The FSS score is the mean of the ratings for the 9 items.

Symptom Ratings: Pain

Pediatric Quality of Life Pain Scale (PedsQL Pain Scale; Gragg et al., 1996; 3 items). The PedsQL Pain Scale measures the impact of pain on quality of life, as rated by the parent or child. High correlations of the PedsQL Pain Scale were found with visual analog scale (VAS) pain intensity ratings obtained from parents, physicians, and patients. Significant correlations also were found between pain ratings and measures of disease activity and functional status.

Pain Intensity Measures (Cohen et al., 2008; Turk & Melzack, 2011). Pain intensity measures are informal measures designed to elicit a rating of pain on a continuous scale such as a 1–10 scale, a location on a line, or the height of a pain thermometer. Specific components of pain can be rated such as intensity, duration, and frequency. Parents and teens can provide ratings independently, allowing for comparison of their perception of the child's pain level.

Pain Location Measures (Cohen et al., 2008; Turk & Melzack, 2011). Pain location measures present the teen with an outline of a body, and the teen indicates the location of the pain by shading in the body region(s) where the pain occurs. Additional information may be provided by using different colors to indicate pain severity (e.g., red = very severe; yellow = moderately severe; green = mild).

Symptom Ratings: Sleep

Pittsburgh Sleep Quality Index-Modified Version (PSQI-MV; Buysse, Reynolds, Monk, Berman, & Kupfer, 1989; 18 items). The PSQI-MV is a measure of sleep characteristics and quality over the past month based on the original PSQI of Buysse et al. (1989). Modifications include removing the six items about sleeping with a partner and providing specific multiple-choice options for all items based directly on ratings listed by Buysse et al. (1989). PSQI-MV items may be rated by either the parent based on the child's sleep or based on the child's self-report. Item content includes bedtime, waking time, time to fall asleep, hours of sleep, difficulty sleeping because of various problems (using the bathroom, snoring, uncomfortable breathing, dreams, pain, etc.), difficulty staying awake, and general rating of sleep quality. Items are rated on a 0–3 scale. PSQI scores fall into several scales, including subjective sleep quality, sleep latency, sleep duration, habitual sleep efficiency, sleep disturbances, use of sleeping medication, daytime dysfunction, and global PSQI score (sum of the 18 items).

Appendix H

Conducting CHIRP in a Group Format

Why Conduct CHIRP in a Group Format?

Although the Children's Health and Illness Recovery Program (CHIRP) was originally designed as an individual intervention with limited family psychoeducation/involvement, the demand for services and subsequent clinical experience has led to increasing the flexibility with which the program can be administered. Obviously, conducting CHIRP in a group format allows for a larger number of patients to be seen simultaneously. Additionally, many, if not most teens seen in CHIRP have become socially isolated and avoidant of peer contact, and the group experience can provide them with a safe and supportive environment in which to increase peer involvement and address their social anxiety. Adolescents referred due to functional disability associated with their chronic illness often engage in avoidant coping strategies and thus are reluctant to engage in social interaction with peers even though they may verbalize not having problems in this arena. Providing intervention in a group format can more directly address this issue.

When bringing up the idea of involving teens in CHIRP in a group format, most of the teens vocalize a strong objection to, if not outright fear of, socializing with other teens or talking about their medical condition with others. However, experience with these groups often reveals that although most teens state that they would feel uncomfortable/inhibited and would not benefit from a group intervention, by the third session participants enjoy meeting with peers who are coping with varied chronic medical conditions and even begin to form friendships that extend beyond the group sessions.

In our experience, once their teens began participating in a CHIRP group, their parents expressed a desire to meet in their own parallel group at the same time as the teens. This has led to conducting CHIRP in parallel teen and parent groups. We have also found it beneficial to have the teens join the parents for a conjoint session on two or three occasions during the course of treatment, consistent with the minimum of three conjoint family sessions when

CHIRP is conducted in an individual/family treatment format. A distinct advantage in working with parents in a group setting is the potential to reduce defensiveness and address dynamics of potential overprotection and enmeshment in a less threatening context.

Furthermore, we have found that the potential for parents to be more responsive to making changes in the parent–teen relationship in order to help their child meet key developmental milestones is often more easily accomplished in a group context. This is a particularly important goal of parenting a teen with a chronic health condition. Developmentally, milestones to be reached during adolescence involve the teen becoming increasingly independent. Improvements in functioning must be made if the teen is to have the experiences and skills necessary to transition to adult life. This development involves the mastery of formative tasks before being able to gain independence from the family system. In our experience, over the course of treatment, parents begin to perceive the skills that their teens learn in CHIRP as essential to meeting these developmental milestones and being able to effectively manage lifestyle decision making appropriate to their medical condition and personal goals. Meeting with parents/guardians in a weekly group format allows for a more in-depth exploration of these issues not so easily engaged in individual sessions.

Sidebar H.1 Reducing Social Isolation in Group-Format CHIRP

Jennifer, a 16-year-old girl with cystic fibrosis stated, "Before the group I was not terribly outgoing. I literally ate lunch with a vending machine. I was not one for confrontation. But after CHIRP I was able to stand up for myself and advocate for things that I need. I could tell people when to back off when something is too much. I didn't just sit there and take it anymore. Really, I made a lot of friends in the group, too. When I came into the group I was scared, not expecting to meet one person I liked. But I came out of that first meeting with a couple of friends, and they even came to my birthday 2 weeks later. It was a really good experience. My advice is just to be yourself. I've got some terribly dark humorous ways and . . . everybody thought it was great. Whether you are funny or shy or whatever . . . just 'do you,' man!"

Clinician's Role

It goes without saying that, in order to effectively conduct the interventions in the CHIRP manualized treatment, which includes administration in a group format, the clinician should be familiar with the psychological impact of pediatric chronic illness on child and adolescent development. In light of the high comorbidity of affective disorders with chronic pediatric illness and painful conditions, you should carefully monitor mood symptomatology and refer the patient for additional individual services if needed. This is particularly important if there is a high risk for self-injurious behavior. It is not uncommon for adolescents to already have an individual therapist when coming to CHIRP group; in such cases, we recommend that the CHIRP clinician obtain a signed release to be able to communicate with the patient's individual therapist and/or physician should any concerns arise. As with any therapeutic relationship, focus on building rapport with patients and managing group dynamics while flexibly applying all components of the CHIRP intervention (i.e., employing fidelity with flexibility in treatment delivery).

When conducting CHIRP utilizing the parallel teen and parent group format, a second clinician (or more) will be necessary if both groups are conducted simultaneously. The clinician conducting the parent group will benefit from experience in working with adults, particularly adults dealing with parenting issues. Furthermore, an in-depth understanding of the considerable stress experienced by parents of children with chronic health conditions is needed so that the clinician understands the forces that may have shaped the difficulties leading to referral. In some cases, a parent may present in the group as so overwhelmed and preoccupied with the demands of their child's illness that they can unwittingly, or even knowingly, dominate group discussion and disrupt the group process. A sensitive and diplomatic handling of such occurrences is essential to making the parent group experience meaningful and effective.

Group Format

Group Orientation

When CHIRP is conducted in a group format, referred participants are seen in the group from intake to the end of CHIRP sessions in order to create an experience that encourages the development of healthy interpersonal bonds and support. For many of the teens seen in CHIRP, and for some parents, this may be their first social experience in some time and they are understandably anxious about feeling comfortable and accepted.

Depending on setting and time factors, the clinician may or may not conduct a full in-depth initial assessment of referrals to CHIRP when it is conducted in a group format. With large numbers of referrals (in our setting we have received up to 40 referrals in a 3-month period), it will likely be much more time- and cost-effective to conduct a combined group intake and orientation session. In a group intake, it is helpful to have parents complete the CHIRP Group Intake Form (Appendix I) in order to obtain basic demographics, necessary information with regard to current functioning, and basic information regarding medical history. This should be supplemented by summary medical information provided by the referring physician.

Even if individual intakes are feasible, a group orientation will be an imperative part of conducting CHIRP in a group format. The group orientation serves as a platform to present an overview of the sessions, a review of the treatment goals, and to foster teen and parent motivation and commitment to completing the CHIRP intervention. During the group orientation, the clinician meets conjointly with parents and teens to discuss the format of the program (e.g., importance of attending the 12 weekly sessions in order to develop a unified skill base), to demystify biases about group sessions (e.g., CHIRP is *not* sitting in a circle and being forced to talk about your most intimate problems), and to gather initial data about functioning and symptomatology via rating scales.

Teen Group

In the initial session, it is important to facilitate group cohesion. Ice-breaker exercises can be extremely helpful to encourage group involvement and engagement. Typically, teens also introduce themselves and are encouraged to share the basis for their referral to CHIRP. However, if teens are not comfortable sharing immediately, do not force them to do so, but rather encourage them to share as they feel more comfortable.

For subsequent sessions, there is a typical format that most clinicians follow. First, clinicians lead a group check-in to assess weekly sleep, physical exercise, and activity (see "CHIRP Session-by-Session," in the Introduction to this Clinician Guide). If the teen indicates that they are having trouble in a particular area, utilize guided exploration to encourage group problem solving. The clinician then asks for volunteers to share their homework while identifying and reinforcing areas of progress. The new lesson for that session is presented to the group, with subsequent group activities designed to provide teens the opportunity to practice the newly learned skills while getting feedback from you and the group. Homework associated with the weekly lesson is then assigned with clear expectations about what should be completed for the following week.

It is helpful to choose closing activities that add levity, encourage group cohesion, and facilitate appropriate social interaction. For example, a commonly used activity in many CHIRP groups is "Good-Stuff Ball." For "Good-Stuff Ball," each teen is encouraged to share an accomplishment from the past week of which they are proud, to set a personal goal for the upcoming week, and to compliment another group member for an act in the group session or an accomplishment. The teen then passes the ball to the group member to whom they directed the compliment, and that teen then repeats the process. We have found this activity to reflect certain aspects of the group process (e.g., mutual respect, level of group cohesion, and level of insight). Finally, if assessment data is to be collected, it is typical to collect such data at the end of the session.

Sidebar H.2 The Good Stuff Ball

When the good stuff ball was thrown to Daryn (a 16-year-old boy with type 1 diabetes) by the CHIRP clinician, the teen stated "I'm proud of myself for getting out of the house and going to play basketball with my friends even though I wasn't feeling all that great." He stated that his goal for the upcoming week was "to check my blood sugar level four times a day, every day of this week." Daryn then turned to Molly (a 15-year-old girl with postconcussive syndrome and chronic headaches) and stated, "I liked how you started our group conversations today . . . you are a good communicator." He then tossed the good stuff ball to Molly, who continued the pattern.

Parent Group

The following are goals of the parent group intervention:

- To provide parents with ongoing education about the skills their teens will be acquiring over the course of the CHIRP intervention;
- To foster an appreciation for the important role parents play in assisting their teen in meeting crucial developmental milestones;
- To provide a supportive environment where parents can discuss and explore their roles in facilitating increased independence in their teen; and
- To expand their awareness of the importance of self-care and modeling effective coping skills for their teen.

Parents of adolescents with chronic illness often experience immense stress from multiple domains. These include taking time off from work to keep multiple medical and therapy appointments; managing the stress and disruption associated with hospitalizations; addressing school attendance and academic needs; and contending with the logistical, financial, and clerical/administrative requirements of insurance, all the while having to attend to the physical and emotional needs of their spouse and the ill teen's siblings. With strong guidance and leadership by the CHIRP clinician, we have found most parent CHIRP groups to be a place where the attendees develop a network in which they can support, encourage, and share openly while learning from one another.

Providing parents with materials covered in the teen group serves to facilitate family out-of-session discussion about the skills learned in the group. Other approaches that may be helpful in the parent group include activities involving role-playing exercises of parent–teen communications and problem-solving strategies.

Sidebar H.3 Communication

At a parent group meeting, a father shared with the group that the 45-minute drive to the CHIRP meetings often resulted in his feeling frustrated that his daughter continued to talk about her school day experiences in a negative light. This was despite his observation that she was actually enjoying more social engagement with her peers. The CHIRP clinician engaged the father in a role-play of the conversation between himself and his daughter, with the father taking the daughter's role. When the CHIRP clinician refrained from being directive and telling the daughter how to fix her problems and instead used more reflective and Socratic comments, the father (in the role of his daughter), chuckled in amusement at his "misguided support" and was speechless.

Conjoint Parent/Teen Sessions

Although conjoint sessions with both teens and parents can be highly effective, they should be used in moderation. The timing of these sessions, especially the first combined session, is crucial. It is important for the teen group to have developed adequate rapport and cohesion, allowing them to comfortably support one another in their communication with the parents. The CHIRP clinician conducting the parent group should instruct the parents to allow the teens to take the lead and guide the conversation. Conjoint sessions are typically held at Sessions 6 and 8 and at the final group meeting. These are noted in the Clinician Guide as "Session Format: *Family-Focused Session*: Meet together with teen and their parent(s)."

Another format to be considered for the combined parent–teen sessions is to have each teen and their parent(s) meet for the first part of the session with the assigned task of problem solving together on a specific topic. Then the family groups are brought together for the second half of the session to share and discuss their experiences. This process is facilitated by having two or more CHIRP clinicians to circulate about the room to help each parent–teen combination with the problem-solving process. When the family groups are brought together, their discussion of their experiences in problem-solving can lead to very spirited and productive conversations about the challenges of becoming aware of and changing ways of communicating and relating that are fostered in CHIRP.

Group Dynamics

As with any group therapy, attention to managing group dynamics is an important factor for group success. It can be challenging for the CHIRP clinician, given the diverse range of medical conditions and personal situations, to validate every group member in a session. For example:

- Some group members may monopolize the session with lengthy presentations of their (the teen's) medical journey, including disclosing personal information that may make other group members uncomfortable.
- Conversely, some group members may be reluctant to share even the most basic of information and personal experiences.
- Other group members may discuss their experiences in highly negative terms that can dampen the group atmosphere.
- Another dynamic occurs when, despite the clinician's best efforts, group members remain silent and reluctant to engage, leading to prolonged and uncomfortable silence.

On the other hand, some teens will serve as positive role models in their participation, enthusiasm, and completion of homework assignments. The gains that these participants make can often motivate others to step up their joining in group interactions and compliance with out-of-group assignments. In the parent group, those who readily grasp the importance of embracing strategies that encourage and support their adolescent's development of independence can serve as role models for parents who tend to be overprotective and enmeshed with their teen. This dynamic can be a powerful experience that is often difficult to duplicate in individual sessions. In the teen group, participants who willingly share and openly participate can create an accepting atmosphere for more reluctant group members.

Research suggests that, to maximize group cohesion and effectiveness, participation should be limited to no more than eight members (Yalom & Leszcz, 2008). With the complexity of concerns and severity of medical conditions, eight participants is likely the maximum number of group members who should be included, even with a co-leader present. Our experience would indicate that a minimum of four participants is desirable. Previous groups have fared quite well with 4–8 group members present. It is important to note that due to the high incidence of avoidant coping we see in many of these youths, many of the teens and parents who are referred for CHIRP group will not attend the group. Thus, even with a large number of referrals, only a fraction of those referrals will express interest in the group and an even smaller percentage will attend the group. However, past experience and empirical data have shown that those who attend CHIRP group benefit and increase functioning. While it may be an option (depending on your clinical setting) to offer individual/family-based CHIRP to those referrals who decline to attend the group format, it generally has been our experience that these referrals would have benefited much more from the social interaction experiences available in the group format. Last, some families who have participated in individual/family-based CHIRP have later requested to join a CHIRP group to get the social interaction experience for their teen, with very positive outcomes.

Employing Media

Media can be used as a supplemental tool for the CHIRP group. Adolescents regularly communicate and engage with multiple media outlets; thus, teens typically pay attention to the messages conveyed in dissemination of media. Media can range from interactive web portals to videos. Videos are often fun interactive tools that can include testimonials or skill-acquisition depictions. We encourage clinicians to use media flexibly during the CHIRP group, in both the teen group and the parent group.

Sidebar H.4 Videos

Before starting the Session 7 discussion on communication, the CHIRP clinician played a video illustrating passive/avoidant, aggressive, and assertive communication. In this video a teen who has chronic pain and dysautonomia is role-playing three different styles of communication in a conversation with her physical therapist. The teen came to her session stating that she wanted to stop seeing the physical therapist because, "She doesn't believe me when I say I am hurting and I need to stop the exercise. She's mean to me and I don't want to go back and work with her. She pushes me too hard." In the video the teen role-plays with her CHIRP clinician an aggressive, passive, and, finally, an assertive approach to having a discussion with the physical therapist as to how the adolescent would like her therapist to be more responsive to her requests when she feels she is being pushed beyond her limits. This exercise leads to a fruitful discussion in the group about more effective and appropriate ways to get their needs met while "avoiding the avoidance cycle."

Group Follow-Up Sessions

Following the conclusion of the formalized CHIRP weekly group, we encourage spaced follow-up or booster sessions to be held to ensure that the teens and parents are maintaining gains obtained throughout the group. Some clinicians offer regular follow-up groups to assess patient functioning and provide guidance for overcoming upcoming barriers; such groups should be strategically placed around predictable stressors. For example, a follow-up group scheduled immediately before the beginning of the school year serves to prepare the teens for reentry into school and remind them how to adaptively cope with impending stress. These groups also serve as a social gathering for teens and parents, which increases social engagement and interaction. The frequency of such groups can be quite flexible and based on accessibility and availability.

Appendix I

CHIRP Group Intake Form

Date: ______________________

Teen name: ______________________________

Date of birth: ________________________

School name: ____________________________

Grade: ______________________

Who lives in the household with the teen?

____

____

____

What are the teen's medical diagnoses, and at what age were they diagnosed?

____

____

____

How do the teen's medical diagnoses impact school attendance/performance?

____

____

____

How do the teen's medical diagnoses impact family relationships?

____

____

____

How do the teen's medical diagnoses impact their social relationships?

____

____

____

Does the teen have any symptoms of anxiety? If so, please explain:

____

____

____

Does the teen have any symptoms of depression? If so, please explain:

____

____

____

Does the teen have any other behavioral/mental health diagnoses? If so, please explain:

____

____

____

Does the teen see a therapist/mental health provider for individual or family therapy, or a psychiatrist for medication management? If yes, please list provider, frequency of appointments, medications, and other relevant information.

____

____

____

Who are the teen's medical providers (doctors, therapists, etc.)? Please list provider name, specialty, and contact information. We may have you sign consent for us to communicate with them as part of CHIRP.

____

____

____

Is there any other information that we should know about the teen to help us in our work together in CHIRP?

____

____

____

Appendix J

CHIRP Outcomes Study Results

Sample demographics

Variable	*N*	Range	Mean	SD
Age	26	11–19	15.46	1.86
Grade	23	6–13	10.04	1.87
GPA	20	2.8–4.0	3.62	0.39
Family income	22	1–11	7.91	3.35

Sex		#
	Male	1
	Female	25
Race		
	White	26
Respondent		
	Mother	24
	Father	1
	Grandmother	1
Medical diagnosis		
	POTS	1
	Dysautonomia	2

	Fibromyalgia	10
	CFS	3
	Chronic headache	8
	CRPS	5
	RSD	2
	RAP	2
	Pseudoseizures	2
DSM Axis I diagnosis		
	Depression	9
	Anxiety	7
	Other Axis 1 diagnosis	16
	Prior psychotherapy	6

	N	Pretreatment Mean	Pretreatment SD	Posttreatment Mean	Posttreatment SD	t (ES)	95% CI
Parent report							
Fatigue (FSS)	26	46.16	10.49	35.31	12.58	3.69*** (0.74)	4.79–16.92
Functioning (FDI)	26	19.77	11.45	12.85	9.56	3.30** (0.66)	2.59–11.24
Pain (PSS)	26	46.87	13.92	32.23	15.46	4.70*** (0.94)	8.22–21.05
Helped symptoms				8.13	2.46		
Helped functioning				8.96	1.27		
Self-report							
Fatigue (FSS)	25	48.12	9.28	31.20	11.83	7.08*** (1.45)	11.98–21.85
Functioning (FDI)	26	23.07	13.33	13.80	10.34	3.50** (0.70)	3.82–14.73
Pain (PSS)	26	45.73	14.30	30.50	12.90	5.09*** (1.02)	9.07–21.39
Helped symptoms				7.21	2.23		
Helped functioning				8.75	1.36		

Note: Mean and standard deviation (SD) values are for 26 subjects who provided both pretreatment and posttreatment data (*N* = 25 for teen report of fatigue). t-test is for primary efficacy analyses comparing treatment completers on pretreatment vs. posttreatment scores. 95% CI is the 95% confidence interval for difference between pretreatment and posttreatment scores. ES is effect size expressed as Cohen's d.

*p<0.05, **p<0.01, ***p<0.001.

CFS, chronic fatigue syndrome; CRPS, complex regional pain syndrome; FDI, Functional Disability Inventory; FSS, Fatigue Severity Scale; POTS, postural orthostatic tachycardia syndrome; PSS, Pain Severity Scale; RAP, recurrent abdominal pain; RSD; reflex sympathetic dystrophy syndrome.

Appendix K

CHIRP Follow-Up Study Results

	Pretreatment			Follow-up			
	N	Mean	SD	*N*	Mean	SD	t-test (df)
Parent report							
Fatigue (FSS)	17	41.41	15.49	17	27.23	18.53	2.61 (16)*
Pain (PSS)	17	51.47	11.55	17	25.47	13.92	9.47 (16)***
Function (FDI)	17	21.94	15.71	17	11.18	10.54	2.55 (16)*
Self-report							
Fatigue (FSS)	14	39.79	11.90	14	27.57	15.42	5.06 (13)***
Pain (PSS)	14	46.07	14.31	14	29.35	18.94	5.44 (13)***
Function (FDI)	13	22.69	9.27	13	12.54	11.69	3.79 (12)**

Note: Pretreatment assessment conducted prior to Session 1 of CHIRP; Follow-up assessment conducted mean of 2.1 years after completion of CHIRP intervention. FDI, Functional Disability Inventory; FSS, Fatigue Severity Scale; PSS, Pain Severity Scale; SD, standard deviation.

*$p<0.05$, **$p<0.01$, ***$p<0.001$.

Appendix L

CHIRP Commitment Form

We are glad that your health care provider has recommended you to the Children's Health and Illness Recovery Program (CHIRP)! We receive referrals of young people who are coping with the challenges of living with a chronic medical condition from all over the region, and we believe this reflects the confidence and positive outcomes that physicians and clinicians have experienced over the years in the patients they have referred.

Our research has shown that teens with chronic medical conditions who complete CHIRP report significant improvements, both at the end of CHIRP and up to 2 years later, in the following areas:

- Decrease in symptoms of fatigue and pain.
- Improvement in sleep.
- Improvement in mood and decreased anxiety.
- Increase in activity level.
- Improvement in confidence in social relationships.
- More likely to return to school and improvement in academic performance.
- Improvement in quality of life for both teen and family.
- Feeling more prepared for the transition to young adult life.

The positive outcomes that have been achieved with CHIRP have resulted in the *Children's Health and Illness Recovery Program (CHIRP): Clinician Guide* and *Children's Health and Illness Recovery Program (CHIRP): Teen and Family Workbook* (that we will use in your treatment) being published by Oxford University Press in their *Programs That Work* books, part of the *Treatments That Work* series aimed at children and families. As a result, CHIRP is being used to help adolescents and families in dealing with the impact of chronic illness in hospitals and health care settings across the country.

Importance of Making the Commitment to CHIRP

Like any treatment, *CHIRP only works if you fully participate in it.* While we realize that there may be challenges to coming to weekly sessions for the 12 weeks needed to help you acquire all of the skills taught in CHIRP, our research and the testimonies of the many teens and families who have benefitted from CHIRP indicate that it is well worth the commitment.

By signing below, you agree to attend all of the CHIRP sessions and perform the activities in the Workbook. Your clinician will sign this form with you to attest to their commitment to providing you with the highest quality, evidence-based interventions to improve your personal functioning and quality of life. We look forward to fulfilling this commitment together!

____

Teen

____

Parent/Guardian

____

CHIRP clinician

Date: ________

Bibliography

Aaltonen, K., Hamalainen, M. L., & Hoppu, K. (2000). Migraine attacks and sleep in children. *Cephalalgia, 20*, 580–584.

Abbott, R. A., Martin, A. E., Newlove-Delgado, T. V., Bethel, A., Thompson-Coon, J., Whear, R., & Logan, S. (2017). Psychosocial interventions for recurrent abdominal pain in childhood. *Cochrane Database Systematic Reviews, 1*, CD010971. doi: 10.1002/14651858.CD010971.pub2

Agoston, A. M., & Sieberg, C. B. (2016, August). Nonpharmacologic treatment of pain. *Seminars in Pediatric Neurology, 23*(3), 220–223.

Amari, A., Slifer, K. J., Sevier, R. C., Spezio, J., & Tucker, C. L. (1998). Using differential reinforcement to treat functional hypophonia in a pediatric rehabilitation patient. *Pediatric Rehabilitation, 2*(2), 89–94.

American Pain Society. (2001). Pediatric chronic pain: A position statement from the American Pain Society. *American Pain Society Bulletin*, Jan/Feb, 10–12.

Anthony, K. K., & Schanberg, L. E. (2005). Pediatric pain syndromes and management of pain in children and adolescents with rheumatic disease. *Pediatric Clinics of North America, 52*(2), 611–639. doi: 10.1016/j.pcl.2005.01.003

Apkarian, A. V., Thomas, P. S., Krauss, B. R., & Szevernyi, N. M. (2001). Prefrontal cortical hyperactivity in patients with sympathetically mediated chronic pain. *Neuroscience Letters, 311*(3), 193–197. doi: 10.1016/S0304-3940(01)02122-X

Baker, J., & Harris, A. (1977). The experimental production of altered physiological states. In W. K. Honig & J. E. R. Staddon (Eds.), *Handbook of operant behavior* (pp. 241–255). Englewood Cliffs, NJ: Prentice Hall.

Banez, G. A., Frazier, T. W., Wojtowicz, A. A., Buchannan, K., Henry, D. E., & Benore, E. (2014). Chronic pain in children and adolescents: 24–42 month outcomes of an inpatient/day hospital interdisciplinary pain rehabilitation program. *Journal of Pediatric Rehabilitation Medicine, 7*(3), 197–206. doi: 10.3233/PRM-140289

Barkley, R. A. (2012). *Barkley Functional Impairment Scale—Children and Adolescents (BFIS-CA)*. New York: Guilford.

Basch, M. C., Chow, E. T., Logan, D. E., Schechter, N. L., & Simons, L. E. (2015). Perspectives on the clinical significance of functional pain syndromes in children. *Journal of Pain Research, 8*, 675–686. doi: 10.2147/JPR.S55586

Beames, L., Sanders, M. R., & Bor, W. (1992). The role of parent training in cognitive behavioral treatment of children's headaches. *Behavioral Psychotherapy, 20*, 167–180. doi: 10.1017/S0141347300016943

Black, W., Cousins, L., Pfeiffer, M., Williams, S., Thomas, S., Kitchen, K., . . . Kashikar-Zuck, S. (2017). Fibromyalgia integrative training for teens (Fit Teens): Results from a pilot randomized trial of integrated exercise and cognitive-behavioral therapy for juvenile fibromyalgia. *Journal of Pain, 18*(4), Supplement, S51. doi.org/10.1016/j.pain.2017.02.197

Brace, M. J., Smith, M. S., McCauley, E., & Sherry, D. D. (2000). Family reinforcement of illness behavior: A comparison of adolescents with chronic fatigue syndrome, juvenile arthritis, and healthy controls. *Journal of Developmental and Behavioral Pediatrics, 21*, 332–339. doi: 10.1097/00004703-200010000-00003

Branson, S. M., & Craig, K. D. (1988). Children's spontaneous strategies for coping with pain. *Canadian Journal of Behavioural Science, 20*, 402–412. doi: 10.1037/h0079937

Bromberg, M. H., Schechter, N. L., Nurko, S., Zempsky, W. T., & Schanberg, L. E. (2014). Persistent pain in chronically ill children without detectable disease activity. *Pain Management, 4*, 211–219. doi: 10.2217/pmt.14.6

Bursch, B., Joseph, M. H., & Zeltzer, L. K. (2003). Pain-associated disability syndrome. In N. L. Schechter, C. B. Berde, & M. Yaster (Eds.), *Pain in infants, children, and adolescents* (pp. 841–848). Philadelphia: Lippincott, Williams, & Williams.

Bursch, B., Walco, G. A., & Zeltzer, L. (1998). Clinical assessment and management of chronic pain and pain associated disability syndrome. *Journal of Developmental and Behavioral Pediatrics, 19*, 45–53. doi: 10.1097/00004703-199802000-00008

Bush, P. J., & Iannotti, R. J. (1990). A children's Health Belief Model. *Medical Care, 28*(1), 69–86. doi: 10.1097/00005650-199001000-00008

Buysse, D. J., Reynolds, C. F., Monk, T. H., Berman, S. R., & Kupfer, D. J. (1989). The Pittsburgh Sleep Quality Index: A new instrument for psychiatric practice and research. *Psychiatry Research, 28*, 193–213. doi: 10.1016/0165-1781(89)90047-4

Carter, B. D., Edwards, J. F., Kronenberger, W. G., Michalczyk, L., & Marshall, G. S. (1995). Case control study of chronic fatigue in pediatric patients. *Pediatrics, 95*, 179–186.

Carter, B. D., Kronenberger, W. G., Crabtree, V. M., Smith, C., Grimes, L. M., McGraw, K., & Baker, J. (2002, April). The Health Experiences and Behaviors Inventory (HEBI): An assessment tool to evaluate psychological factors in physical symptom presentation in pediatric patients. Paper presented at the 2002 Great Lakes Regional Meeting on Child Health Psychology, Milwaukee, WI.

Carter, B. D., Kronenberger, W. G., Cruce, S. E., Mizell, D., Threlkeld, B. M., Brady, C. E., & Jones, L. C. (2015). Factors associated with drop out versus completion of a manualized treatment for pediatric chronic pain. *Clinical Practice in Pediatric Psychology, 3*(4), 327–339. doi: 10.1037/cpp0000119

Carter, B. D., Kronenberger, W. G., Edwards, J. F., Marshall, G. S., Schikler, K. N., & Causey, D. L. (1999). Psychological symptoms in chronic fatigue and juvenile rheumatoid arthritis. *Pediatrics, 103*(5), 975–979.

Carter, B. D., Kronenberger, W. G., Fernander, A., & McGraw, K. (2004, April). The Juvenile Health Experiences & Behaviors Inventory (JHEBI): Evaluation of the psychological dimensions of pediatric illness. Paper presented at the 2004 National Conference on Child Health Psychology, Charleston, SC.

Carter, B. D., Kronenberger, W. G., & King, A. (2006, April). Parental and child health beliefs: Relationship to medical utilization in pediatric health care. Paper presented at the 2006 National Conference on Child Health Psychology, Gainesville, FL.

Carter, B. D., Kronenberger, W. G., Threlkeld, B., Townsend, A., & Pruitt, A. (2013). The Children's Health & Illness Recovery Program (CHIRP): Feasibility and preliminary efficacy in a clinical sample of adolescents with chronic pain and fatigue. *Clinical Practice in Pediatric Psychology, 1*(2), 184–195. doi: 10.1037/cpp0000012

Carter, B. D., Schultz, K. V., Gilbert, E. A., Kronenberger, W. K., & Scott, E. L. (2018, April). Case series with a group teen/parent intervention for chronic illness coping and pain: Evolution of the CHIRP intervention. Poster presented at the 2018 National Conference on Pediatric Psychology, Orlando, FL.

Center for Functional Assessment Research. (1998). *Guide for the Uniform Data Set for Medical Rehabilitation for Children (WeeFIM)*. Version 5.0. Inpatient. Buffalo, NY: Center for Functional Assessment Research, Uniform Data System for Medical Rehabilitation, State University of New York.

Chalder, T., Godfrey, E., Ridsdale, L., King, M., & Wessely, S. (2003). Predictors of outcome in a fatigued population in primary care following a randomized controlled trial. *Psychological Medicine, 33*(2), 283–287. doi: 10.1017/S0033291702007006

Charmandari, E., Kino, T., Souvatzoglou, E., & Chrousos, G. P. (2003). Pediatric stress: Hormonal mediators and human development. *Hormone Research, 59*(4), 161–179. doi: 10.1159/000069325

Christie, D., & Wilson, C. (2005). CBT in paediatric and adolescent health settings: A review of practice-based evidence. *Developmental Neurorehabilitation, 8*(4), 241–247. doi: 10.1080/13638490500066622

Claar, R. L., & Walker, L. S. (2006). Functional assessment of pediatric pain patients: Psychometric properties of the functional disability inventory. *Pain, 121*, 77–84. doi: 10.1016/j.pain.2005.12.002

Claar, R. L., Walker, L. S., & Smith, C. A. (1999). Functional disability in adolescents and young adults with symptoms of irritable bowel syndrome: The role of academic, social, and athletic competence. *Journal of Pediatric Psychology, 24*(3), 271–280. doi: 10.1093/jpepsy/24.3.271

Cohen, L. L., Lemanek, K., Blount, R. L., Dahlquist, L. M., Lim, C. S., Palermo, T. M., . . . Weiss, K. E. (2008). Evidence-based assessment of pediatric pain. *Journal of Pediatric Psychology, 33*(9), 939–955.

Covelman, K., Scott, S., Buchanan, B., & Rossman, F. (1990). Pediatric pain control: A family systems model. In D. C. Tyler & E. J. Krane (Eds.), *Advances in pain research and therapy* (pp. 225–236). New York: Raven Press.

Crabtree, V. M., Krishna, J., & Gozal, D. (2008). Insomnia due to medical condition. In J. W. Winkelman et al. (Eds.), *Casebook of sleep medicine* (pp. 57–60). New York: American Academy of Sleep Medicine.

Crombez, G., Bijttebier, P., Eccleston, C., Mascagni, T., Mertens, G., Goubert, L., & Verstraeten, K. (2003). The child version of the Pain Catastrophizing Scale (PCS-C): A preliminary validation. *Pain, 104*, 639–646. doi: 10.1016/S0304-3959(03)00121-0

Dahl, J., Wilson, K. G., & Nilsson, A. (2004). Acceptance and commitment therapy and the treatment of persons at risk for long-term disability resulting from stress and pain symptoms: A preliminary randomized trial. *Behavior Therapy, 35*, 785–802. doi: 10.1016/S0005-7894(04)80020-0

Degotardi, P J., Klass, E. S., Rosenberg, B. S., Fox, D. G., Gallelli, K. A., & Gottlieb, B. S. (2006). Development and evaluation of a cognitive-behavioral intervention for juvenile fibromyalgia. *Journal of Pediatric Psychology, 31*, 714–723. doi: 10.1093/jpepsy/jsj064

Dunn-Geier, B. J., McGrath, P. J., Rourke, B. P., Latter, J., D'Astous, J. (1986). Adolescent chronic pain: The ability to cope. *Pain*, 26, 23–32. doi: 10.1016/0304-3959(86)90170-3

DuPaul, G. J., Power, T. J., & Shapiro, E. S. (2017). Schools and reintegration into schools. In M. C. Roberts & R. G. Steele (Eds.), *Handbook of pediatric psychology* (5th ed., pp. 580–593). New York: Guilford.

Eccleston, C., & Clinch, J. (2007). Adolescent chronic pain and disability: A review of the current evidence in assessment and treatment. *Paediatrics & Child Health*, 12, I(2), 117–120. https://doi.org/10.1093/pch/12.2.117

Eccleston, C., Jordan, A. L., & Crombez, G. (2005). The impact of chronic pain on adolescents: A review of previously used measures. *Journal of Pediatric Psychology, 31*(7), 684–697. doi: 10.1093/jpepsy/jsj061

Eccleston, C., Malleson, P. M., Clinch, J., Connell, H., & Sourbut, C. (2003). Chronic pain in adolescents: Evaluation of a programme of inter-disciplinary cognitive behaviour therapy. *Archives of Disease in Childhood, 88*, 881–885.

Eccleston, C., Morley, S., Williams, A., Yorke, L., & Mastroyannopoulou, K. (2002). Systematic review of randomized controlled trials of psychological therapy for chronic pain in children and adolescents, with a subset meta-analysis of pain relief. *Pain, 99*, 156–165. doi: 10.1016/S0304-3959(02)00072-6

Eccleston, C., Palermo, T. M., Williams, A. C., Lewandowski Holley, A., Morley, S., Fisher, E., & Law, E. (2014). Psychological therapies for the management of chronic and recurrent pain in children and adolescents. *Cochrane Database of Systematic Reviews, 5*, CD003968. doi: 10.1002/14651858.CD003968.pub4

Eiser, C. (1997). Effects of chronic illness on children and their families. *Advances in Psychiatric Treatment, 3*(4), 204–210. doi: 10.1192/apt.3.4.204

Finney, J. W., Lemanek, K. L., Cataldo, M. F., Katz, H. P., & Fuqua, R. W. (1989). Pediatric psychology in primary health care: Brief targeted therapy for recurrent abdominal pain. *Behavior Therapy, 20*, 283–291.

Flor, H., Birbaumer, N., & Turk, D. C. (1990). The psychobiology of chronic pain. *Advances in Behavioral Research and Therapy, 12*, 47–84. doi: 10.1016/0146-6402(90)90007-D

Folkman, S., Lazarus, R. S., Gruen, R. J., & DeLongis, A. (1986). Appraisal, coping, health status, and psychological symptoms. *Journal of Personality and Social Psychology, 50*(3), 571–579. doi: 10.1037/0022-3514.50.3.571

Fordyce, W. E. (1976). *Behavioral methods for chronic pain and illness*. St. Louis: Mosby.

Gaab, J., Huster, D., Peisen, R., Engert, V., Heitz, V., Schad, T., . . . Ehlert, U. (2002). Hypothalamic-pituitary-adrenal axis reactivity in chronic fatigue syndrome and health under psychological, physiological, and pharmacological stimulation. *Psychosomatic Medicine, 64*(6), 951–962. doi: 10.1097/01.PSY.0000038937.67401.61

Garber, J., Walker, L. S., & Zeman, J. (1991). Somatization symptoms in a community sample of children and adolescents: Further validation of the Children's Somatization Inventory. *Psychological Assessment, 3*(4), 588–595. doi: 10.1037/1040-3590.3.4.588

Garber, J., Zeman, J., & Walker, L. S. (1990). Recurrent abdominal pain in children: Psychiatric diagnoses and parental psychopathology. *Journal of the American Academy of Child & Adolescent Psychiatry, 29*(4), 648–656. doi: 10.1097/00004583-199007000-00021

Garralda, M. (1996). Somatisation in children. *Journal of Child Psychology and Psychiatry, 37*(1), 13–33. doi: 10.1111/j.1469-7610.1996.tb01378.x

Garralda, M., & Chandler, T. (2005). Practitioner review: Chronic fatigue syndrome in childhood. *Journal of Child Psychology and Psychiatry, 46*(11), 1143–1151. doi: 10.1111/j.1469-7610.2005.01424.x

Gidron, Y., McGrath, P. J., & Goodday, R. (1995). The physical and psychosocial predictors of adolescents' recovery from oral surgery. *Journal of Behavioral Medicine, 18*, 385–399. doi: 10.1007/BF01857662

Gill, A. C., Dosen, A., & Ziegler, J. B. (2004). Chronic fatigue syndrome in adolescents: A follow-up study. *Archives of Pediatrics & Adolescent Medicine, 158*(3), 225–229. doi: 10.1001/archpedi.158.3.225

Goodman, J. E., & McGrath, P. A. (1991). The epidemiology of pain in children and adolescents: A review. *Pain, 46*, 247–264. doi: 10.1016/0304-3959(91)90108-A

Gragg, R. A., Rapoff, M. A., Danovsky, M. B., Lindsley, C. B., Varni, J. W., Waldron, S. A., & Bernstein, B. H. (1996). Assessing chronic musculoskeletal pain associated with rheumatic disease: Further validation of the Pediatric Pain Questionnaire. *Journal of Pediatric Psychology, 21*(2), 237–250. doi: 10.1093/jpepsy/21.2.237

Guite, J. W., Logan, D. E., Simons, L. E., Blood, E. A., & Kerns, R. D. (2011). Readiness to change in pediatric chronic pain: Initial validation of adolescent and parent versions of the Pain Stages of Change Questionnaire. *Pain, 152*(10), 2301–2311. doi.org/10.1016/j.pain.2011.06.019

Hayes, S. C., Strosahl, K. D., & Wilson, K. G. (1999). *Acceptance and commitment therapy: An experiential approach to behavior change.* New York: Guilford.

Hechler, T., Ruhe, A. K., Schmidt, P., Hirsch, J., Wager, J., Dobe, M., & Zernikow, B. (2014). Inpatient-based intensive interdisciplinary pain treatment for highly impaired children with severe chronic pain: Randomized controlled trial of efficacy and economic effects. *Pain, 155*(1), 118–128. doi: 10.1016/j.pain.2013.09.015

Herbert, M. (1994). Etiological considerations. In T. M. Ollendick, N. J. Kin, & W. Yule (Eds.), *International handbook of phobic anxiety disorders in children and adolescents* (pp. 3–20). New York: Plenum Press.

Herman, C., Kim, M., & Blanchard, E. B. (1995). Behavioral and prophylactic pharmacological intervention studies of pediatric migraine: An exploratory meta-analysis. *Pain, 60,* 239–256. doi: 10.1016/0304-3959(94)00210-6

Hicks, C. L., von Baeyer, C. L., & McGrath, P. J. (2006). Online psychological treatment for pediatric recurrent pain: A randomized evaluation. *Journal of Pediatric Psychology, 31,* 724–736. doi: 10.1093/jpepsy/jsj065

Holden, E. W., Deichmann, M. M., & Levy, J. D. (1999). Empirically supported treatments in pediatric psychology: Recurrent pediatric headache. *Journal of Pediatric Psychology, 24*(2), 91–109. doi: 10.1093/jpepsy/24.2.91

Hunfeld, J. A. M., Perquin, C. W., Duivenvoorden, H. J., Hazebroek-Kampschreur, A. A. J. M., Passchler, J., van Suijlekom-Smit, L. W. A., & van der Wouden, J. C. (2001). Chronic pain and its impact on quality of life in adolescents and their families. *Journal of Pediatric Psychology, 26,* 145–153. doi: 10.1093/jpepsy/26.3.145

Huntley, E. D., Campo, J. V., Dahl, R. E., & Lewin, D. S. (2007). Sleep characteristics of youth with functional abdominal pain and a healthy comparison group. *Journal of Pediatric Psychology, 32,* 938–949. doi: 10.1093/jpepsy/jsm032

Hutchison, W. D., Davis, K. D., Lozano, A. M., Tasker, R. R., & Dostrovsky, J. O. (1999). Pain-related neurons in the human cingulate cortex. *Nature and Neuroscience, 2*(5), 403–405. doi: 10.1038/8065

Hyams, J. S., & Hyman, P. E. (1998). Recurrent abdominal pain and the biopsychosocial model of medical practice. *Journal of Pediatrics, 133*(4), 473–478. doi: 10.1016/S0022-3476(98)70053-8

Hyman, P. E., Bursch, B., Sood, M., Schwankovsky, L., Cocjin, J., & Zeltzer, L. K. (2002). Visceral pain-associated disability syndrome: A descriptive analysis. *Journal of Pediatric Gastroenterology and Nutrition, 35,* 663–668.

Hysing, M., Sivertsen, B., Stormark, K. M., Elgen, I., & Lundervold, A. J. (2009). Sleep in children with chronic illness and the relation to emotional and behavioral problems: A population-based study. *Journal of Pediatric Psychology, 34*(6):665–670. doi: 10.1093/jpepsy/jsn095. doi: 10.1093/jpepsy/jsn095

Janicke, D. M., & Finney, J. W. (1999). Empirically supported treatments in pediatric psychology: Recurrent abdominal pain. *Journal of Pediatric Psychology, 34*(2), 115–127. doi: 10.1093/jpepsy/24.2.115 doi: 10.1093/jpepsy/24.2.115

Jensen, M. P., Turner, J. A., & Roman, J. M. (2001). Changing in beliefs, catastrophizing, and coping are associated with improvement in multidisciplinary pain treatment. *Journal of Consulting and Clinical Psychology, 69*(4), 665–662. doi: 10.1037/0022-006X.69.4.655

Kahana, S., Drotar, D., & Frazier, T. (2008). Meta-analysis of psychological interventions to promote adherence to treatment in pediatric chronic health conditions. *Journal of Pediatric Psychology, 33*(6), 590–611. doi: 10.1093/jpepsy/jsm128

Kashikar-Zuck, S., Cunningham, N., Sil, S., Bromberg, M. H., Lynch-Jordan, A. M., . . . Arnold, L. M. (2014). Long-term outcomes of adolescents with juvenile-onset fibromyalgia in early adulthood. *Pediatrics, 133*, e592–e600. doi: 10.1542/peds.2013-2220

Kashikar-Zuck, S., Goldschneider, K. R., Powers, S. W., Vaught, M. H., & Hersey, A. D. (2001). Depression and functional disability in chronic pediatric pain. *Clinical Journal of Pain, 17*, 341–349. doi: 10.1097/00002508-200112000-00009

Kashikar-Zuck, S., Swain, N. F., Jones, B. A., & Graham, T. B. (2005). Efficacy of cognitive-behavioral intervention for juvenile primary fibromyalgia syndrome. *Journal of Rheumatology, 32*(8), 594–602.

Kazak A. E., Simms, S., & Rourke M. T. (2002). Family systems practice in pediatric psychology. *Journal of Pediatric Psychology, 27*, 13–43. doi: 10.1093/jpepsy/27.2.133

King, S., Chambers, C. T., Huguet, A., MacNevin, R. C., McGrath, P. J., Parker, L., & MacDonald, A. J. (2011). The epidemiology of chronic pain in children and adolescents revisited: A systematic review. *Pain, 152*(12), 2729–2738. doi: 10.1016/j.pain.2011.07.016

Kopp, M., Richter, R., Rainer, J., Kopp-Wilfling, P. Rumpold, G., & Walter, M. H. (1995). Differences in family functioning between patients with chronic headache and patients with chronic low back pain. *Pain, 63*, 219–224. doi: 10.1016/0304-3959(95)00045-T

Kristjansdottir, G. (1997). Prevalence of pain combinations and overall pain: A study of headache, stomach pain and back pain among schoolchildren. *Scandinavian Journal of Socialized Medicine, 25*(1), 58–63. doi: 10.1177/140349489702500112

Kroener-Herwig, B., & Denecke, H. (2002). Cognitive-behavioral therapy of pediatric headache: Are there differences in the efficacy between a therapist-administered group training and a self-help format? *Journal of Psychosomatic Research, 53*, 1107–1114. doi: 10.1016/S0022-3999(02)00345-8

Kroll, K. (2019). *Telepsychotherapy via Home-Based Videoconferencing.* Presentation at the Department of Psychiatry and Behavioral Medicine Grand Rounds, Medical College of Wisconsin.

Kronenberger, W. G. (2003). *Child Observed Coping Scale.* Unpublished test manual.

Kronenberger, W. G., & Dunn, D. W. (2009). Conversion reaction. In B. Maria (Ed.), *Current management in child neurology* (4th ed., pp. 544–549). Gainesville, FL: Decker.

Kronenberger, W. G., Carter, B. D., Morrow, C., Stewart, J., Martin, K., & Sender, L. (1993, April). *Stress, coping, and psychological adjustment of children undergoing bone marrow transplantation.* Poster presented at the Fourth Florida Conference on Child Health Psychology.

Kronenberger, W. G., Carter, B. D., Stewart, J., Morrow, C., Martin, K., Gowan, D., & Sender, L. (1996). Psychological adjustment of children in the pretransplant phase of bone marrow transplantation: Relationships with parent distress, parent stress, and child coping. *Journal of Clinical Psychology in Medical Settings, 3*(4), 319–335. doi: 10.1007/BF01994017

Kronenberger, W. G., & Meyer, R. G. (2001). *Child clinician's handbook* (2nd ed., pp. 134–145). Needham Heights, MA: Allyn & Bacon.

Krupp, L. B., LaRocca, N. G., Muir-Nash, J., & Steinberg, A. D. (1989). The fatigue severity scale: Application to patients with multiple sclerosis and systemic lupus erythematosus. *Archives of Neurology, 46*(10), 1121–1123. doi: 10.1001/archneur.1989.00520460115022

Lautenbacher, S., Kundermann, B., & Krieg, J. (2006). Sleep deprivation and pain perception. *Sleep Medicine Reviews, 10*(5), 357–369. doi: 10.1016/j.smrv.2005.08.001

Law, E. F., Noel, M., Nagel, M. S., & Dahlquist, L. M. (2017). Chronic and recurrent pain. In M. C. Roberts & R. G. Steele (Eds.), *Handbook of pediatric psychology* (5th ed., pp. 134–145). New York: Guilford.

Lewandowski, A. S., Palermo, T. M., De la Motte, S., & Fu, R. (2010). Temporal daily associations between pain and sleep in adolescents with chronic pain versus healthy adolescents. *Pain, 151*(1), 220–225. doi: 10.1016/j.pain.2010.07.016

Lewandowski, A. S., Palermo, T. M., Stinson, J., Handley, S., & Chambers, C. T. (2010). Systematic review of family functioning in families of children and adolescents with chronic pain. *Journal of Pain, 11*(11), 1027–1038. doi: 10.1016/j.jpain.2010.04.005

Lewin, D. S., & Dahl, R. E. (1999). The importance of sleep in the management of pediatric pain. *Journal of Developmental and Behavioral Pediatrics, 20*(4), 244–252. doi: 10.1097/00004703-199908000-00007

Liakopoulou-Kairis, M., Alifieraki, T., Protagora, D., Korpa, T., Kondyli, K., Dimosthenous, E., . . . Kovanis, T. (2002). Recurrent abdominal pain and headache: Psychopathology, life events and family functioning. *European Child and Adolescent Psychiatry, 11*(3), 115–122. doi: 10.1007/s00787-002-0276-0

Lipani, T. A., & Walker, L. S. (2005). Children's appraisal and coping with pain: Relations to maternal ratings of worry and restriction in family activities. *Journal of Pediatric Psychology, 31*(7), 667–673. doi: 10.1093/jpepsy/jsj038

Logan, D. E., Carpino, E. A., Chiang, G., Condon, M., Firn, E., Gaughan, V. J., & Berde, C. B. (2012). A day-hospital approach to treatment of pediatric complex regional pain syndrome: Initial functional outcomes. *Clinical Journal of Pain, 28*(9),766–774. doi: 10.1097/AJP.0b013e3182457619

Logan, D. E., & Scharff, L. (2005). Relationships between family and parent characteristics and functional abilities in children with recurrent pain syndromes: An investigation of moderating effects on the pathway from pain to disability. *Journal of Pediatric Psychology, 30*(8), 698–707. doi: 10.1093/jpepsy/jsj060

Long, A. C., Krishnamurphy, V., & Palermo, T. M. (2008). Sleep disturbances in school-age children and chronic pain. *Journal of Pediatric Psychology, 33*(3), 258–268. doi: 10.1093/jpepsy/jsm129

Lynch, A. M., Kashikar-Zuck, S., Goldschneider, K. R., & Jones, B. A. (2006). Psychosocial risks for disability in children with chronic back pain. *Journal of Pain, 7*(4), 244–251. doi: 10.1016/j.jpain.2005.11.001

MacAllister, W. S., Christodoulou, C., Troxell, R, Milazzo, M., Block, P., Preston, T. E., . . . Krupp, L. B. (2009). Fatigue and quality of life in pediatric multiple sclerosis. *Multiple Sclerosis, 15*(12),1502–1508. doi: 10.1177/1352458509345902

Maynard, C. S., Amari, A., Wieczorek, B., Christensen, J. R., & Slifer, K. J. (2010). Interdisciplinary behavioral rehabilitation of pediatric pain-associated disability: Retrospective review of an inpatient treatment protocol. *Journal of Pediatric Psychology, 35*(2), 128–137. doi: 10.1093/jpepsy/jsp038

McCarthy, M. C., Bastiani, J., & Williams, L. K. (2016). Are parenting behaviors associated with child sleep problems during treatment for acute lymphoblastic leukemia? *Cancer Medicine. 5*(7), 1473–1480. doi: 10.1002/cam4.727.

McCracken, L. (1998). Learning to live with pain: Acceptance of pain predicts adjustment in persons with chronic pain. *Pain, 74*(1), 21–27. doi: 10.1016/S0304-3959(97)00146-2

Meltzer, L. J., Logan, D. E., & Mindell, J. A. (2005). Sleep patterns in female adolescents with chronic musculoskeletal pain. *Behavioral Sleep Medicine, 3*(4), 193–208. doi: 10.1207/s15402010bsm0304_2

Meltzer, L. J., & Montgomery-Downs, H. E. (2011). Sleep in the family. *Pediatric Clinics of North America, 58*(3), 765–774. doi: 10.1016/j.pcl.2011.03.010.

Miller, V. A., Palermo, T. M., Powers, S. W., Scher, M. S., & Hershey, A. D. (2003). Migraine headaches and sleep disturbances in children. *Headache, 43*(4), 362–368. doi: 10.1046/j.1526-4610.2003.03071.x

Mitchell, D. K., Kopel, S. J., Williams, B., Cespedes, A., & Bruzzese, J. M. (2015). The association between asthma and sleep in urban adolescents with undiagnosed asthma. *Journal of School Health, 85*(8), 519–526. doi: 10.1111/josh.12277.

Moss-Morris, R., Sharon, C., Tobin, R., & Baldi, J. C. (2005). A randomized controlled graded exercise trial for chronic fatigue syndrome: Outcomes and mechanisms of change. *Journal of Health Psychology, 10*(2), 245–259. doi: 10.1177/1359105305049774

Naidoo, P., & Pillay, Y. G. (1994). Correlations among general stress, family environment, psychological distress, and pain experience. *Perceptual and Motor Skills*, 78, 1291–1296. doi: 10.2466/pms.1994.78.3c.1291

Noll, R. B., LeRoy, S., Bukowski, W. M., Rogosch, F. A., & Kulkarni, R. (1991). Peer relationships and adjustment in children with cancer. *Journal of Pediatric Psychology, 16*(3), 307–326. doi: 10.1093/jpepsy/16.3.307

Palermo, T. (2012). *Cognitive-behavioral therapy for chronic pain in children and adolescents*. New York: Oxford.

Palermo, T. M. (2000). Impact of recurrent and chronic pain on child and family daily functioning: A critical review of the literature. *Journal of Developmental and Behavioral Pediatrics, 21*, 58–69. doi: 10.1097/00004703-200002000-00011

Palermo, T. M., Eccleston, C., Lewandowski, A. S., de C. Williams, A. C., & Morley, S. (2010). Randomized controlled trials of psychological therapies for management of chronic pain in children and adolescents: An updated meta-analytic review. *Pain, 148*, 387–397. doi: 10.1016/j.pain.2009.10.004

Palermo, T. M., & Kiska, R. (2005). Subjective sleep disturbances in adolescents with chronic pain: Relationship to daily functioning and quality of life. *Journal of Pain, 6*, 201–207. doi: 10.1016/j.jpain.2004.12.005

Palermo, T. M., Wilson, A. C., Peters, M., Lewandowski, A., & Somhegyi, H. (2009). Randomized controlled trial of an Internet-delivered family cognitive-behavioral therapy intervention for children and adolescents with chronic pain. *Pain, 146*(1-2), 205–213. doi.org/10.1016/j.pain.2009.07.034.

Payne, B., & Norfleet, M. (1986). Chronic pain and the family: A review. *Pain, 26*(1), 1–22. doi: 10.1012/0304-3959(86)90169-7

Perquin, C. W., Hazebroek-Kampschreur, A. A., Hunfeld, J. A., Bohnen, A. M., van Suijlekom-Smit, L. W., Passchier, J., & Van der Wouden, J. C. (2000). Pain in children and adolescents: A common experience. *Pain, 87*(2), 51–58. doi: 10.1016/S0304-3959(00)00269-4

Peterson, C. C., & Palermo, T. M. (2004). Parental reinforcement of recurrent pain: The moderating impact of child depression and anxiety on functional disability. *Journal of Pediatric Psychology, 29*(5), 331–341. doi: 10.1093/jpepsy/jsh037

Pinquart, M., & Teubert, D. (2012). Academic, physical, and social functioning of children and adolescents with chronic physical illness: A meta-analysis. *Journal of Pediatric Psychology 37*(4), 376–389. doi: 10.1093/jpepsy/jsr106

Prochaska, J. O., & DiClemente, C. C. (2005). The transtheoretical approach. In J. C. Norcross & M. R. Goldfried (Eds.), *Handbook of psychotherapy integration* (pp. 147–171). New York: Oxford University Press.

Rabbitts, J. A., Holley, A. L., Groenewald, C. B., & Palermo, T. M. (2016). Association between widespread pain scores and functional impairment and health-related quality of life in clinical samples of children. *Journal of Pain, 17*(6), 678–684. doi: 10.1016/j.jpain.2016.02.005

Reed-Knight, B., Van Tilburg, M. A. L., Levy, R. L., Langer, S. L., Romano, J., Burwinkle, T. M., . . . Feld, A. D. (2017). Maladaptive coping and depressive symptoms partially explain the association between family stress and pain-related distress in youth with IBD. *Journal of Pediatric Psychology, 43*(1), doi: 10.1093/jpepsy/jsx082.

Reynolds, C. R., & Kamphaus, R. W. (2015). *Behavior Assessment System for Children Manual* (3rd ed.). Bloomington, MN: Pearson.

Rodgers, C., Norville, R., Taylor, O., Poon, C., Hesselgrave, J., Gregurich, M. A., & Hockenberry, M. (2012). Children's coping strategies for chemotherapy-induced nausea and vomiting. *Oncology Nursing Forum, 39*(2), 202–209. doi: 10.1188/12.ONF.202-209

Roehrs, T., Hyde, M., Blaisdell, B., Greenwald, M., & Roth, T. (2006). Sleep loss and REM sleep loss are hyperalgesic. *Sleep*, 29, 145–151. doi: 10.1093/sleep/29.2.145

Roth-Isigkeit, A., Thyen, U., Stoven, H., Schwarzenberger, J., & Schmucker, P. (2005). Pain among children and adolescents: Restrictions in daily living and triggering factors [Electronic version]. *Pediatrics, 115*, e152–e162. doi: 10.1542/peds.2004-0682

Prochaska, J. O., & DiClemente, C. C. (2005). The transtheoretical approach. In J. C. Norcross & M. R. Goldfried (Eds.), *Handbook of psychotherapy integration* (2nd ed., pp. 147–171). New York: Oxford University Press.

Reed-Knight, B., van Tilburg, M. A., Levy, R. L., Langer, S. L., Romano J. M., Murphy, T. B., . . . Feld, A. D. (2018). Maladaptive coping and depressive symptoms partially explain the association between family stress and pain-related distress in youth with IBD. *Journal of Pediatric Psychology, 43*(1), 94–103. doi.org/10.1093/jpepsy/jsx082

Rizou, I., De Gucht, V., Papavasiliou, A., & Maes, S. (2016). The contribution of illness perceptions to fatigue and sleep problems in youngsters with epilepsy. *European Journal of Paediatric Neurology, 20*(1), 93–99. doi: 10.1016/j.ejpn.2015.10.001. Epub 2015 Oct 17.

Robin, A. L., & Foster, S. L. (1989). *Negotiating parent-adolescent conflict: A behavioral-family systems approach.* New York: Guilford.

Sanders, M. R., Shepherd, R. W., Cleghorn, G., & Woolford, H. (1994). The treatment of recurrent abdominal pain in children: A controlled comparison of cognitive-behavioral family intervention and standard pediatric care. *Journal of Consultation Clinical Psychology, 62*(2), 306–314. doi: 10.1037/0022-006X.62.2.306

Schanberg, L. E., Anthony, K. K., Gil, K. M., & Maurin, E. C. (2003). Daily pain and symptoms in children with polyarticular arthritis. *Arthritis and Rheumatism, 48*(5), 1390–1397. doi: 10.1002/art.10986

Schanberg, L. E., Anthony, K. K., Gil, K. M., Lefebvre, J. C., Kredich, D. W., & Macharoni, L. M. (2001). Family pain history predicts child health status in children with chronic rheumatic disease. *Pediatrics, 108*, E47. doi: 10.1542/peds.108.3.e47

Scharff, L., Langan, N., Rotter, N., Scott-Sutherland, J., Schenck, C., Tayor, N., . . . Bruce, M. (2005). Psychological, behavioral, and family characteristics of pediatric patients with chronic pain. *Clinical Journal of Pain, 21*(5), 432–438. doi: 10.1097/01.ajp.0000130160.40974.f5

Schmidt-Wilcke, T., & Clauw, D. J. (2011). Fibromyalgia: From pathophysiology to therapy. *National Review of Rheumatology, 7*, 518–527. doi: 10.1038/nrrheum.2011.98

Seligman, M. E. P. (1992). *Helplessness: On depression, development, and death.* New York: WH Freeman.

Shapiro, E. S., & Manz, P. H. (2004). Collaborating with schools in the provision of pediatric psychological services. In R. T. Brown (Ed.), *Handbook of pediatric psychology in school settings* (pp. 49–64). Mahwah, NJ: Erlbaum.

Siegel, L. J., & Smith, K. E. (1989). Children's strategies for coping with pain. *Pediatrician, 16*(1–2), 110–118.

Simons, L. E., Sieberg, C. B., Pielech, M., Conroy, C., & Logan, D. E. (2013). What does it take? Comparing intensive rehabilitation to outpatient treatment for children with significant pain-related disability. *Journal of Pediatric Psychology, 38*(2), 213–223. doi: 10.1093/jpepsy/jss109

Sivertsen, B., Hysing, M., Elgen, I., Stormark, K. M., & Lundervold, A. J. (2009). Chronicity of sleep problems in children with chronic illness: A longitudinal population-based study. *Child and Adolescent Psychiatry and Mental Health, 273*(1), 22. doi: 10.1186/1753-2000-3-22.

Smith, M., & Carter, B. D. (2004). Chronic fatigue syndrome in adolescence. In L. Jason, P. Fennell, & R. Taylor (Eds.), *Handbook of chronic fatigue syndrome* (2nd ed.; pp. 693–712) New York: Wiley & Sons.

Snodgrass, K., Harvey, A, Scheinberg, A., & Knight, S. (2015). Sleep disturbances in pediatric chronic fatigue syndrome: A review of current research. *Journal of Clinical Sleep Medicine, 11*(7), 757–764. doi: 10.5664/jcsm.4854.

Spirito, A., Stark, L. J., & Williams, C. (1988). Development of a brief coping checklist for use with pediatric populations. *Journal of Pediatric Psychology, 13*(4), 555–574. doi: 10.1093/jpepsy/13.4.555

Stang, P. E., & Osterhaus, J. T. (1993). Impact of migraine in the United States: Data from the National Health Interview Survey. *Headache, 33*(1), 29–35. doi: 10.1111/j.1526-4610.1993.hed3301029.x

Sterr, A., & Freivogel, S. (2003). Motor-improvement following intensive training in low- functioning chronic hemiparesis. *Neurology, 61*(6), 842–844. doi: 10.1212/WNL.61.6.842

Stinson, J. N., Hayden, J. A., Ahola-Kohut, S., Soobiah, C., Cartwright, J., Weiss, S. K., & Witmans, M. B. (2014). Sleep problems and associated factors in children with juvenile idiopathic arthritis: A systematic review. *Pediatric Rheumatology Online Journal, 12*(19). doi: 10.1186/1546-0096-12-19.

Stulemeijer, M., de Jong, W. A. M., Fiselier, T. J. W., Hoogveld, S. W. B., & Bleijenberg, G. (2005). Cognitive behaviour therapy for adolescents with chronic fatigue syndrome: Randomized controlled trial. *British Medical Journal, 14*, 330. doi: 10.1136/bmj.38301.587106.63

Sumpter, R. E., Dorris, L., Kelly, T., & McMillan, T. M. (2013). Pediatric sleep difficulties after moderate-severe traumatic brain injury. *Journal of the International Neuropsychological Society, 19*(7), 829–834. doi: 10.1017/S1355617713000465.

Suris, J. C., Michaud, P. A., & Viner, R. (2004). The adolescent with a chronic condition. Part I: Developmental issues. *Archives of Disease in Childhood, 89*(10), 938–942. doi: 10.1136/adc.2003.045369

Szigethy, E., Kenney, E., Carpenter, J., Hardy, D. M., Fairclough, D., Bousvaros, A., . . . DeMaso, D. R. (2007). Cognitive-behavioral therapy for adolescents with inflammatory bowel disease and subsyndromal depression. *Journal of the American Academy of Child & Adolescent Psychiatry, 46*(10), 1290–1298. doi.org/10.1097/chi.0b013e3180f6341f

Thompson, R. J., Gil, K. M., Burbach, D. J., Keith, B. R., & Kinney, T. R. (1993). Role of child and maternal processes in the psychological adjustment of children with sickle cell disease. *Journal of Consulting and Clinical Psychology, 61*(3), 468–474. doi: 10.1037//0022-006X.61.3.468

Tsai, S. Y., Labyk, S. E., Richardson, L. P., Lentz, M. J., Brandt, P. A., Ward, T. M., . . . Landis, C. A. (2008). Brief report: Actigraphic sleep and daytime naps in adolescent girls with chronic musculoskeletal pain. *Journal of Pediatric Psychology, 33*(3), 307–311. doi: 10.1093/jpepsy/jsm117

Turk, D. C., & Melzack, R. (2011). *Handbook of pain assessmen* (3rd ed.). New York: Guilford.

Valrie, C. R., Bromberg, M. H., Palermo, T., & Schanberg, L. E. (2013). A systematic review of sleep in pediatric pain ppulations. *Journal of Developmental & Behavioral Pediatrics, 34*(2), 120–128. doi: 10.1097/dbp.0b013e31827d5848

van den Brink, M., Bandell-Hoekstra, E. N. G., & Huijer Abu-Saad, H. (2001). The occurrence of recall bias in pediatric headache: A comparison of questionnaire and diary data. *Headache, 41*(1), 11–20. doi: 10.1046/j.1526-4610.2001.111006011.x

Van Slyke D. A., & Walker, L. S. (2006). Mothers' responses to adolescent's pain. *Clinical Journal of Pain, 22*(4), 387–391. doi: 10.1097/01.ajp.0000205257.80044.01

Varni, J. W., Burwinkle, T. M., & Szer, I. S. (2004). The PedsQL Multidimensional Fatigue Scale in pediatric rheumatology: Reliability and validity. *Journal of Rheumatology, 31*(12), 2494–2500.

Vater, L., Hermetet-Lindsay, K., Delahanty, S., Carter, B., Woods, D., & Bhatia, P. (2019, April). Tic Talks at 5 o'clock: Expanding the use of the Chronic Health Illness Recovery Program to meet the needs of adolescents with tic disorders. Poster presented at the Society of Pediatric Psychology Annual Conference, New Orleans, LA.

Vervoort, T., Goubert, L., Eccleston, C., Bijttebier, P., & Crombez, G. (2006). Catastrophic thinking about pain is independently associated with pain severity, disability and somatic complaints in school children with chronic pain. *Journal of Pediatric Psychology, 31*(7), 674–683. doi: 10.1093/jpepsy/jsj059

Viner, R., Gregorowski, C., Wine, M., Bladen, D., Fisher, M., Miller, M., & El Neil, S. (2004). Outpatient rehabilitative treatment of chronic fatigue syndrome (CFS/ME). *Archives of Disease in Childhood, 89*(7), 615–619. doi: 10.1136/adc.2003.035154

Wagner, J. L., Ferguson, P. L., & Smith, G. (2012). The relationship of coping behaviors to depressive symptoms in youth with epilepsy: An examination of caregiver and youth proxy report. *Epilepsy and Behavior, 24*(1), 86–92. doi: 10.1016/j.yebeh.2012.02.017

Walker, L. S., Claar, R. L., & Garber, J. (2002). Social consequences of children's pain: When do they encourage symptom maintenance? *Journal of Pediatric Psychology, 27*(8), 689–698. doi: 10.1093/jpepsy/27.8.689

Walker, L. S., Garber, J., & Greene, J. W. (1993). Psychosocial correlates of recurrent childhood pain: A comparison of pediatric patients with recurrent abdominal pain, organic illness, and psychiatric disorders. *Journal of Abnormal Psychology, 102*(2), 248–258. doi: 10.1037/0021-843X.102.2.248

Walker, L. S., & Greene, J. W. (1991). The functional disability inventory: Measuring a neglected dimension of child health status. *Journal of Pediatric Psychology, 16*(1), 39–58. doi: 10.1093/jpepsy/16.1.39

Walker, L. S., Williams, S. E., Smith, C. A., Garber, J., Van Slyke, D. A., & Lipani, T. A. (2006). Parent attention versus distraction: Impact on symptom complaints by children with and without chronic functional abdominal pain. *Pain, 122*(1–2), 43–52. doi: 10.1016/j.pain.2005.12.020

Walker, L. S., & Zeman, J. L. (1992). Parental response to child illness behavior. *Journal of Pediatric Psychology, 17*(1), 49–71. doi: 10.1093/jpepsy/17.1.49

Wallander, J. L., & Varni, J. W. (1998). Effects of pediatric chronic physical disorder on child and family adjustment. *Journal of Child Psychology and Psychiatry and Allied Disciplines, 39*(1), 29–46. doi: 10.1111/1469-7610.00302

Walter, L. M., Nixon, G. M., Davey, M. J., Downie, P. A., & Horne, R. S. (2015). Sleep and fatigue in pediatric oncology: A review of the literature. *Sleep Medicine Review, 24*, 71–82. doi: 10.1016/j.smrv.2015.01.001.

Weiss, K. E., Hahn, A., Wallace, D. P., Biggs, B., Bruce, B. K., & Harrison, T. E. (2013). Acceptance of pain: Associations with depression, catastrophizing, and functional disability among children and adolescents in an interdisciplinary chronic pain rehabilitation program. *Journal of Pediatric Psychology, 38*(7), 756–765. doi: 10.1093/jpepsy/jst028

Whitehead, W. E., Crowell, M. D., Heller, B. R., Robinson, J. C., Schuster, M. M., & Horn, S. (1994). Modeling and reinforcement of the sick role during childhood predicts adult illness behavior. *Psychosomatic Medicine, 56*(6), 541–550. doi: 10.1097/00006842-199411000-00010

Williams, S. E., & Zahka, N. E. (2017). *Treating somatic symptoms in children and adolescents.* New York: Guilford.

Wolfe, F. (2009). Fibromyalgianess. *Arthritis and Rheumatology, 61*(6), 715–716. doi: 10.1002/art.24553

Wolfe, F., Hauser, W., Hassett, A. L., Katz, R. S., & Walitt, B. T. (2011). The development of fibromyalgia–I: Examination of rates and predictors in patients with rheumatoid arthritis. *Pain, 152*(2), 291–299. doi: 10.1016/j.pain.2010.09.027

Woolf, C. J. (2011). Central sensitization: Implications for the diagnosis and treatment of pain. *Pain, 152*(3 Suppl), S2–S15. doi: 10.1016/j.pain.2010.09.030

Wright, B., Ashby, B., Beverley, D. Calvert, E., Jordan, J., Miles, J., . . . Williams, C. A feasibility study comparing two treatments for chronic fatigue syndrome in adolescents. (2005). *Archives of Diseases in Children, 90*(4), 369–372. doi: 10.1136/adc.2003.046649

Wysocki, T., Harris, M. A., Buckloh, L. M., Mertlich, D., Lochrie, A. S., Mauras, N., & White, N. H. (2007). Randomized trial of behavioral family systems therapy for diabetes: Maintenance of effects on diabetes outcomes in adolescents. *Diabetes Care, 30*(3), 555–560. doi: 10.1177/0145445505284275

Wysocki, T., Harris, M. A., Buckloh, L. M., Mertlich, D., Lochrie, A. S., Taylor, A., . . . White, N. H. (2006). Effects of behavioral family systems therapy for diabetes on adolescents' family relationships, treatment adherence, and metabolic control. *Journal of Pediatric Psychology, 31*(9), 928–938. doi: 10.1093/jpepsy/jsj098

Wysocki, T., Harris, M. A., Greco, P., Bubb, J., Danda, C. E., Harvey, L. M., . . . White, N. H. (2000). Randomized, controlled trial of behavior therapy for families of adolescents with insulin-dependent diabetes mellitus. *Journal of Pediatric Psychology, 25*, 23–33.

Wysocki, T., Harris, M., Greco, P., Mertlich, D., & Buckloh, L. (2001). *Behavioral family systems therapy (BFST) for adolescents with a chronic illness* (Unpublished treatment manual).

Wysocki, T., Miller, K., Greco, P., Harris, M. A., Harvey, L., Taylor, A., . . . White, N. H. (1999). Behavior therapy for families of adolescents with diabetes: Effects on directly observed family interactions. *Behavior Therapy, 301*(3), 507–525. doi: 10.1016/S0005-7894(99)80022-7

Yalom, I. D., & Leszcz, M. (2008). *The theory and practice of group psychotherapy* (5th ed.). New York: Basic Books.

Zeltzer, L., Bursch, B., & Walco, G. (1997). Pain responsiveness and chronic pain: A psychobiological perspective. *Journal of Developmental and Behavioral Pediatrics, 18*(6), 413–422.

Zeltzer, L. K., Tsao, J. C., Bursch, B., & Myers, C. D. (2006). Introduction to the special issues on pain: From pain to pain-associated disability syndrome. *Journal of Pediatric Psychology, 31*(7), 661–666. doi: 10.1093/jpepsy/jsj053

Zhou, E. S., Vrooman, L. M., Manley, P. E., Crabtree, V. M., & Recklitis, C. J. (2017). Adapted delivery of cognitive-behavioral treatment for insomnia in adolescent and young adult cancer survivors: A pilot study. *Behavioral Sleep Medicine, 15*(4), 288–301. doi: 10.1080/15402002.2015.1126597

About the Authors

Bryan D. Carter, PhD, is Professor in the Division of Child and Adolescent Psychiatry and Psychology, Department of Pediatrics, University of Louisville School of Medicine and Service Chief of the Pediatric Consultation-Liaison Service with Norton Children's Hospital. He is also Associate Division Chief, Training Director of the postdoctoral fellowship in pediatric psychology, and directs the Children's Health and Illness Recovery Program (CHIRP) services with the Bingham Clinic.

William G. Kronenberger, PhD, is Professor of Clinical Psychology in Psychiatry at Indiana University School of Medicine and Chief of the Pediatric Psychology Testing Clinic at Riley Hospital for Children. Dr. Kronenberger is also the Executive Vice Chair of the Department of Psychiatry and Director of the Section of Psychology at Indiana University School of Medicine.

Eric L. Scott, PhD, is Associate Professor of Pediatrics and Anesthesiology at the University of Michigan Medical School and director of the Michigan Pediatric and Adolescent Interdisciplinary Network (MiPAIN), an interdisciplinary pediatric pain clinic at Michigan Medicine and CS Mott Children's Hospital.

Christine E. Brady, PhD, is Associate Professor in the Division of Child and Adolescent Psychiatry and Psychology, Department of Pediatrics, University of Louisville School of Medicine and Assistant Director of the Pediatric Consultation-Liaison Service with Norton Children's Hospital. She is also co-director of the Gender Clinic through pediatric endocrinology at the University of Louisville.